TEACHING TO
MULTIPLE INTELLIGENCES

IN THE
FRENCH CLASSROOM

Activities and presentations for use with

HEATH

Caroline Marion
Edgerton Public Schools
Edgerton, Minnesota

McDougal Littell

Evanston, Illinois • Boston • Dallas

D.C. Heath and Company
A Division of Houghton Mifflin Company

Copyright © 1997 by D.C. Heath and Company, a Division of Houghton Mifflin Company.

Printed in the United States of America

International Standard Book Number: 0-669-44648-3

4   5   6   7   8   –DAA–   04   03   02   01   00

Contents

INTRODUCTION

Have you ever wondered why one student might react positively to a certain activity or presentation while another student might react negatively? It was not until I studied Howard Gardner's theory of multiple intelligences that I fully understood why students react so differently. In his book, *Frames of Mind,* Gardner defines seven separate areas of intelligence: **bodily-kinesthetic, spatial, musical, logical-mathematical, interpersonal, intrapersonal,** and **linguistic.** We all have these seven areas of intelligence but in different combinations of strengths. Everyone has at least one area of strength or high intelligence. It is through our area of high intelligence that we learn best. We can also best interest our students in learning if we target <u>their</u> areas of high intelligence. (I've found that targeting students' intelligences is an excellent way to help reduce discipline problems.)

By targeting each intelligence at least once a week in the classroom, we help each individual "shine," boost self-esteem, and encourage success for all students. It is important to let our students know that we value all seven intelligences and that we need to exercise our whole brain. You'll find that the more intelligences you target in each activity, the more students you can interest or motivate.

You have probably noticed that one of the strengths of *Discovering French* is that it targets many intelligences: the **bodily-kinesthetic,** through TPR activities; the **spatial,** through illustrations and videos; the **logical-mathematical,** through critical thinking activities; the **interpersonal,** through pair and group activities; the **intrapersonal,** through the **À votre tour** sections (self-expression); and the **linguistic,** through writing, reading, speaking and listening activities.

The activities that follow provide you with additional material that is coded so you can see at a glance which intelligences are targeted. As you read the following brief definitions of the seven intelligences, you will probably recognize some of your strengths as well as those of your students.

— Caroline Marion

BODILY-KINESTHETIC We see this intelligence in mimes, dancers, actors and athletes who have the ability to exercise their bodies in skillful ways. Another aspect of the **bodily-kinesthetic** intelligence is the ability to handle objects skillfully (inventors, mechanics and engineers).

A student who has a high **bodily-kinesthetic** intelligence may be good at charades, sports or may enjoy disassembling mechanical objects. Sometimes these students have a hard time sitting still in class. TPR works well for them because they learn best by DOING.

> ☑ *NOTE:* If you are having discipline problems with a class, take time to figure out what intelligences you are working with. If it is the **bodily-kinesthetic,** you probably need to add more physical activity to your routine. (TPR came to my rescue when I had a very hyperactive group.)

SPATIAL We easily recognize the **spatial** intelligence in artists, sculptors and photographers, who have the ability to produce a pictorial likeness of what they see, feel or experience. This intelligence also includes the ability to form pictures in the mind as daydreamers and inventors do. Another aspect of spatial intelligence is the ability to visualize objects from different perspectives as chess players and geometry students do.

Students who are **spatially** intelligent may like to draw or design things. They might also enjoy daydreaming. They have a strong visual memory and learn best through the use of colorful visuals.

> ☑ *NOTE:* You may encounter some resistance from students when you assign them a drawing activity. Just let them know that it's important that we exercise all of our intelligences. The class will also enjoy seeing the different drawing styles unique to each student. A drawing activity will also give the artistic student a chance to shine.

MUSICAL   Our **musical** intelligence enables us to enjoy music through awareness of rhythm, pitch, tone and musical patterns of sound. Pianists, singers and other musicians not only have the ability to appreciate music but also are able to reproduce sounds. Composers use their musical intelligence to create their own kind of music. Students who have a high **musical** intelligence may enter your room humming or whistling. They may be in chorus or band and may learn songs easily. (Have these students help you with some of the musical activities in this book.)

 NOTE: I have found that a French class is often composed of many musical students. It is no doubt the musical sound of the French language that interests many in studying this beautiful language. So rest assured that learning information set to music will be a hit with most of your students!

LOGICAL-MATHEMATICAL   We see this intelligence at work in computer programmers, accountants, lawyers, nurses, doctors, scientists and engineers. The **logical-mathematical** intelligence includes the ability to work with numbers, to solve problems using math and logic, to recognize patterns and to see connections between unlike things.

Students with a high **logical-mathematical** intelligence may enjoy organizing and categorizing things, working with numbers and problem solving. They may want an explanation of how things work ("What makes it rain?").

INTERPERSONAL   Good friends, social workers and counselors often have a high **interpersonal** intelligence which enables them to communicate well with others and to understand how others feel. This intelligence also includes the ability to detect others' true intentions and to react according to this information. Being able to work cooperatively with others is another aspect of this intelligence.

Students who have a high **interpersonal** intelligence enjoy learning by interacting with others (cooperative learning). They may be good peer tutors. Paired and group activities work well with these students.

 INTRAPERSONAL This intelligence helps us understand and express our inner feelings. It also enables us to think in different ways (imagining, predicting, evaluating). Writers, religious workers and entrepreneurs use this intelligence in their work.

Students with a high **intrapersonal** intelligence are often self-confident, self-motivated and not afraid to be different. They may like to express their opinions and may prefer to work alone. (Independent study projects work well with these students.)

 LINGUISTIC It is our **linguistic** intelligence that helps us learn a language by enabling us to hear and repeat the different sounds and rhythms of words, to understand word meanings and use words correctly. Debaters, comedians, teachers and students use this intelligence to influence, to humor, to teach and to learn.

 NOTE: Students with high linguistic intelligence have an advantage in school, since teachers and books tend to target the linguistic intelligence through reading, writing and lecturing.

Many students who excel in school have a high **linguistic** intelligence. Their strong verbal memory helps them memorize long lists of information for test-taking. They are often good at playing trivia games and may like to talk or read.

Teaching to multiple intelligences provides many different entry points for learning. The chart on page 6, from Thomas Armstrong's *Multiple Intelligences in the Classroom* (1994, Association for Supervision and Curriculum Development) provides a concise summary of the teaching activities, materials and strategies most appropriate to successful teaching to each intelligence.

The French classroom can provide an environment that builds inclusion by addressing all potentials for learning, and offers options for success for all students. Although "seven intelligences" are most frequently discussed, this is of course a simplification of the many possible ways of apprehending and learning. It is an easy way to focus on differences in learning styles, and to begin to create activities that encourage successful language learning.

 RESOURCES:

Frames of Mind by Howard Gardner; *Awakening Your Child's Natural Genius, Multiple Intelligences in the Classroom,* and *Encouraging Your Child's Personal Learning Style: In Their Own Way* by Thomas Armstrong; *Seven Ways of Teaching* by David Lazear; *The Everyday Genius* by Peter Kline; *Is the Left Brain Always Right?* Cherry/Godwin/Staples; "How Are You Smart?" Carlson/Marion/Van Westen.

A Summary of the "Seven Ways of Teaching"

INTELLIGENCE:	Teaching Activities Examples	Teaching Materials Examples	Instructional Strategies
LINGUISTIC	Lectures, discussions, word games, storytelling, choral reading, journal writing, etc.	Books, tape recorders, typewriters, stamp sets, books on tape, etc.	Read about it, write about it, talk about it, listen to it.
LOGICAL-MATHEMATICAL	Brain teasers, problem solving, science experiments, mental calculation, number games, critical thinking, etc.	Calculators, math manipulatives, science equipment, math games, etc.	Quantify it, think critically about it, conceptualize it.
SPATIAL	Visual presentations, art activities, imagination games, mind-mapping, metaphor, visualization, etc.	Graphs, maps, video, LEGO sets, art materials, optical illusions, cameras, picture library, etc.	See it, draw it, visualize it, color it, mind-map it.
BODILY-KINESTHETIC	Hands-on learning, drama, dance, sports that teach, tactile activities, relaxation exercises, etc.	Building tools, clay, sports equipment, manipulatives, tactile learning resources, etc.	Build it, act it out, touch it, get a "gut feeling" of it, dance it.
MUSICAL	Superlearning, rapping, songs that teach.	Tape recorder, tape collection, musical instruments	Sing it, rap it, listen to it.
INTERPERSONAL	Cooperative learning, peer tutoring, community involvement, social gatherings, simulations, etc.	Board games, party supplies, props for role plays, etc.	Teach it, collaborate on it, interact with respect to it.
INTRAPERSONAL	Individualized instruction, independent study, options in course of study, self-esteem building, etc.	Self-checking materials, journals, materials for projects, etc.	Connect it to your personal life, make choices with regard to it.

©D.C. Heath and Company, a Division of Houghton Mifflin Company.

UNITÉ 1   QUI SUIS-JE?

1. LES PROFESSIONS   (Unit 1 Lesson 1 p. 37)

These activities target several intelligences. The **interpersonal** intelligence is activated as students work in pairs. The use of dialog targets the **linguistic** intelligence. The **logical-mathematical** intelligence is challenged as students try to guess their profession. The **spatial** intelligence is activated as students pretend to be famous professional persons.

■ To Drill *Les professions*

After you have presented the material on page 37, reinforce the vocabulary with this drill. Make a copy of the list of professions that follows Cut out these words. Then tape one on the back of each student so they cannot see what their profession is. Divide the class into pairs (or a group of three if you have an uneven number of students). Have students quiz their partners to find out what their profession is.

Write the following dialog on the blackboard and practice it with the students before they question their partners. Students must ask at least one question about what a person does (**«Est-ce que je travaille dans un bureau?»**) before asking what the profession is (**«Est-ce que je suis secrétaire?»**).

STUDENT A: **Est-ce que je travaille dans un bureau? (une pharmacie, un théâtre, un hôpital)**
STUDENT B: **Non, tu ne travailles pas dans un bureau.**
STUDENT A: **Est-ce que je travaille dans un hôpital?**
STUDENT B: **Oui, tu travailles dans un hôpital.**
STUDENT A: **Est-ce que je suis docteur?**
STUDENT B: **Non, tu n'es pas docteur.**
STUDENT A: **Est-ce que je suis infirmière?**
STUDENT B: **Oui, tu es infirmière.**

Other phrases students might use:

Est-ce que j'utilise un ordinateur?
Est-ce que je porte de nouveaux vêtements?
Est-ce que je prends beaucoup de photos?
Est-ce que j'aide les malades?
Est-ce que je fais des additions?
Est-ce que j'ai du talent artistique?

When students find out their identity, they should switch roles and ask questions about their identity. (Allow students to refer to vocabulary on p. 37 of the text.)

LIST OF PROFESSIONS

un(e) dentiste

un médecin

un docteur

un infirmier (une infirmière)

un ingénieur

un pharmacien (une pharmacienne)

un programmeur (une programmeuse)

un technicien (une technicienne)

un informaticien (une informaticienne)

un avocat (une avocate)

un vendeur (une vendeuse)

un homme (une femme) d'affaires

un(e) comptable

un employé (une employée) de bureau

un patron (une patronne)

un(e) secrétaire

un acteur (une actrice)

un(e) cinéaste

un(e) photographe

un(e) journaliste

un écrivain

un dessinateur (une dessinatrice)

un mannequin

2. LES NATIONALITÉS, LES PROFESSIONS ET LES PRÉSENTATIONS (Unit 1 Lesson 1 pp. 33, 36–38)

These activities target several intelligences. The **interpersonal** intelligence is activated as students work in pairs. The use of dialog targets the **linguistic** intelligence. The **logical-mathematical** intelligence is challenged as students try to guess their profession. The **spatial** intelligence is activated as students pretend to be famous professional persons.

■ To Drill *Les nationalités, les professions et les présentations*

For this drill, have students work with the same partners they had for Activity 1. Have each student choose to be a famous professional (using the list in the textbook on page 37). Partners take turns introducing each other to the class. When the class hears the name, they try to identify the nationality and profession.

Write the following structured dialog on the blackboard and have students follow this when doing their presentations. Practice the model dialog with them first.

STUDENT A: **Classe, je voudrais vous présenter <u>Shakespeare</u>.**
CLASS: **Enchantés.**
STUDENT B *(Shakespeare):* **Enchanté.**
CLASS *(or an individual student):* **Vous êtes américain?**
STUDENT B: **Non, je ne suis pas américain.**
CLASS: **Vous êtes anglais?**
STUDENT B: **Oui, je suis anglais.**
CLASS: **Vous êtes écrivain?**
STUDENT B: **Oui, je suis écrivian.**

When all presentations have been finished, walk around the class, pointing to various students. Ask the class, «**Comment s'appelle-t-il?**» Class (or an individual) responds: «**Il s'appelle <u>Shakespeare</u>**» (or whatever his identity was). Then you ask, «**Que fait-il?**» Class responds: «**Il est écrivain.**»

3. LA PERSONNALITÉ   (Unit 1 Lesson 2 p. 48)

These activities target the **bodily-kinesthetic** intelligence using TPR to teach vocabulary. The **musical** intelligence is activated through singing. The **linguistic** and **interpersonal** intelligences are targeted as students circulate asking each other questions.

■ To Drill *Vocabulaire: La personnalité*

To present the vocabulary on page 48, begin by introducing the masculine forms of the adjectives using TPR. You might use the gestures suggested below or assign a word to each student and have him or her think up an appropriate gesture. You then say the words one at a time, giving the gesture at the same time. (Whichever student is to give the gesture should give it after you say the word.) The class repeats the word and the gesture. Repeat the word and corresponding gesture again three times and have the class repeat the word and gesture each time. Then go on to the next word, continuing the drill in the same manner until all words have been drilled. (If students made up their own gestures, ask each one to give the gesture and then call on someone in the class to give the verbal response.) Finally, say the words one at a time and ask the class to respond with the corresponding gesture. Tell students you will keep repeating the word until you see all students doing the appropriate gesture.

SUGGESTED GESTURES

ambitieux   act out climbing a ladder

consciencieux   furrow brow and place hand on forehead as if thinking

curieux   look from side to side as if peaking around a corner

ennuyeux   yawn as if bored

généreux   act as if you are handing out something to several people

sérieux   put on a very serious expression

heureux   smile

malheureux   frown

paresseux   slouch and sigh

actif   twirl index finger rapidly in the air

imaginatif   close eyes as if daydreaming

impulsif   put your thumb on your wrist as if taking your pulse

intuitif   snap fingers as if you've suddenly thought of something

naïf   shrug shoulders and look around as if asking "What do I do?"

sportif   pretend to be throwing a ball

mignon   put your chin in the palms of your hands and smile

intellectuel   adjust your glasses or pretend to put on glasses

naturel   take a deep breath and exhale slowly

ponctuel   point to watch

spirituel   raise index finger above head as if making a chalk mark (gesture for "chalk one up")

musicien   pretend to be playing the violin

To teach the different feminine and masculine pronunciations of these adjectives, teach students the words set to music (see next page). If you are not a good singer, have some of your musical students prepare this song to present to the class.

After the song has been presented, divide the class into two groups. Have one group sing the «**Il est...**» part, have the other group sing the «**Elle est...**» part. Have students use the gestures for the words as they sing (thus acting out the song). After the class has sung the song, have them switch parts and sing the song again.

Make copies of the question sheet that follows and hand them out to your students. Have them write their answers for each question. Then ask students to stand and circulate, asking their classmates no more than two questions each. When students have found "yes" answers for every question (or have questioned everyone), they may sit down. They should note on their papers the names of students answering "yes" to their questions. When several students are seated, ask everyone to sit down. Then begin asking students to share their information by asking: «**Qui est ambitieux?**» Students should respond: «**Jack est ambitieux.**» or «**Marie est ambitieuse**» etc. Continue asking questions in this manner until you've covered all questions.

Il est curieux!

Il est cur - i - eux. Elle est cur - i - euse.

Il est im - pul - sif. Elle est im - pul - sive.

Il est très mig - non. Elle est très mig - nonne.

Il est ponc - tu - el. Elle est ponc - tu - elle.

Il est mu - si - cien. Elle est mu - si - cienne.

Je m'appelle _____

1. Est-ce que tu es ambitieux (ambitieuse)?

    _____

2. Est-ce que tu es curieux (curieuse)?

    _____

3. Est-ce que tu es généreux (généreuse)?

    _____

4. Est-ce que tu es impulsif (impulsive)?

    _____

5. Est-ce que tu es ponctuel (ponctuelle)?

    _____

6. Est-ce que tu es musicien (musicienne)?

    _____

7. Est-ce que tu es imaginatif (imaginative)?

    _____

8. Est-ce que tu es spirituel (spirituelle)?

    _____

9. Est-ce que tu es sportif (sportive)?

    _____

10. Est-ce que tu es consciencieux (consciencieuse)?

    _____

4. LES EXPRESSIONS AVEC *FAIRE*   (Unit 1 Lesson 3 pp. 58–59)

These activities target the **bodily-kinesthetic** intelligence with a charades game. The **intrapersonal** intelligence is activated through self-expression as students act out sentences. The **spatial** intelligence is activated when students draw sketches of their charade sentences.

■ To Drill *Les expressions avec* faire

After you have introduced the material on pp. 58–59, play a game of charades. Make a copy of the charades sentences on the next page. Cut out sentences and hand one to each student. Have students take turns acting out their sentences. You might act out the first sentence as the model.

After all students have acted out their sentences, ask an individual, **«Qu'est-ce que Paul a fait?»** Students should respond with a statement about whatever Paul acted out. Example: **«Il a fait du ski.»** (Responses should use **il** or **elle** as the subject.) If a student hesitates with a response, have the class give gestures as clues. If the student called upon still hesitates, call on the entire class to give a group response. Continue asking questions about the rest of the students: **«Qu'est-ce que Marie a fait?»**

Give each student a sheet of white or light-colored construction paper (8 1/2 x 11) and some non-toxic color markers. Ask students to illustrate their charades sentence. On the sketch side of their paper, have them write in large letters the subject pronoun used in their sentence. On the back side, have students write the entire charade sentence in large letters.

When all students have finished drawing their sketches, collect them and show them to the class one at a time. Challenge the students to give you the exact sentence that appears on the back of the sketch.

Use these visuals as flash cards to drill this vocabulary. Later post them on the bulletin board with the title **Les expressions avec faire.** (You will need these visuals for Activity 5.)

CHARADES SENTENCES USING EXPRESSIONS WITH "FAIRE"

1. Tu fais un sandwich.

2. Tu fais tes devoirs.

3. Il fait une promenade.

4. Elle fait attention.

5. Nous faisons un voyage.

6. Vous faites la vaisselle.

7. Elles font du français.

8. Ils font du ski.

9. Tu fais de la photo.

10. Elles font de la gymnastique.

11. Il fait du français.

12. Elle fait ses devoirs.

13. Nous faisons une promenade.

14. Vous faites attention.

15. Elles font la cuisine française.

16. Ils font la vaisselle.

17. Elle fait les courses.

18. Tu fais du jogging.

19. Il fait du golf.

20. Elle fait de la natation.

21. Nous faisons du ski.

22. Vous faites de la photo.

23. Vous faites une omelette.

24. Ils font les courses.

25. Vous faites du ski.

5. LES QUESTIONS AVEC INVERSION   (Unit 1 Lesson 3 pp. 60–61)

This activity targets these intelligences: the **spatial** (with visuals), the **linguistic** (with questions and answers), and the **interpersonal** (with a group activity).

■ To Drill *Les questions avec inversion*

After you have covered the material on pp.60–61, use this drill to challenge students to make up questions using inversion. Use the visuals your students created in Activity 4. Give one visual to each student. Ask a few students to make a question (using inversion) out of the statement on the back of the visual. These students call on someone in the class to answer their questions.

Students should hold visuals up so all can see.

> STUDENT A: **Fait-il une promenade?**
> STUDENT B: **Oui, il fait une promenade.**

Some questions will require a change of subject.

> STUDENT A: **Fais-tu tes devoirs?**
> STUDENT B: **Oui, je fais mes devoirs.** or **Non, je ne fais pas mes devoirs.**

Point to one of the sketches and ask a question using an interrogative expression and inversion.

> TEACHER: **Que fait-elle?**
> STUDENT A: **Elle fait ses devoirs.**

Have a few students hold up their sketches for the class to see and ask the question: **«Que fait-elle?»** (or **«Que font-ils?»**). Students should use the pronoun on the front of their sketch in the question.

> STUDENT A: **Que font-elles?**
> STUDENT B: **Elles font les courses.**

Write the following interrogative expressions on the blackboard:

Où?

Quand?

Avec qui?

Pourquoi?

Que?

Then ask a student who speaks French fairly well to show his or her picture to the class. Have the class ask this student questions about the picture using some of the interrogative expressions listed on the board. Students should, of course, use inversion in their questions and may use the subject **tu**. The student responds with **je** and makes up logical answers.

EXAMPLE: *Student A shows a picture of someone skiing.*
STUDENT B ASKS: **Que fais-tu?**
STUDENT A RESPONDS: **Je fais du ski.**
STUDENT C: **Quand fais-tu du ski?**
STUDENT A: **Je fais du ski en hiver.**
OTHER STUDENTS ASK QUESTIONS: **Avec qui fais-tu du ski? Pourquoi fais-tu du ski? Où fais-tu du ski?**

Now divide your class into groups of four or five. One by one each student shows his or her picture to the group. Each member of the group must make up a question (using an interrogative expression and inversion) to ask the student showing the picture. The student showing the picture makes up a logical response. When he or she has answered a question from each group member, another student holds up a picture and responds to the questions of the group. Students continue this activity until all group members have been questioned.

Have groups exchange visuals when they are finished. If all groups are not ready to exchange visuals, approach a group that is ready and ask them questions about one of the group members. Ask when, why, where he or she does what is on the visual (**«Quand fait-il du ski?»**). (Find out who has been listening.) When all groups are ready, continue with a second round of questioning. This time have students ask questions using the subject pronoun that is written on the visual.

EXAMPLE A:	*Student A shows the visual*	**Elles font de la gymnastique.**
	STUDENT B ASKS:	**Que font-elles?**
	STUDENT A RESPONDS:	**Elles font de la gymnastique.**
EXAMPLE B:	*Student A shows the visual*	**Vous faites attention.**
	STUDENT B ASKS:	**Que faites-vous?**
	STUDENT A RESPONDS:	**Nous faisons attention.**

When students have finished the second drill, you might have them exchange visuals one more time if you feel they are maintaining an interest in this activity.

6. LE VERBE *VENIR;* LA CONSTRUCTION *VENIR DE* + INFINITIF
(Unit 1 Lesson 4 pp. 68–69)

This activity targets the **linguistic** intelligence through writing and speaking. The **logical-mathematical** intelligence is challenged to make a connection as clues are given.

■ To Drill *Le verbe* venir *et la construction* venir de + *infinitif*

Before beginning this activity, go over the material on pp. 68–69. Then write the following sentences on the blackboard.

Je viens de l'école.
Je viens d'écouter le professeur.

Then ask each student to make up two similar sentences. One statement should say he or she is coming from a certain place. The other statement should say he has just done something.

Next, have half the class read their statement about where they've been. **(Je viens de la plage.)** Each student in this group takes turns reading their statement and the class tries to guess what it is that each student just did.

EXAMPLE 1: STUDENT A: **Je viens de la plage.**
STUDENT B: **Tu viens de nager?**
STUDENT A: **Oui, je viens de nager.**

When the first half of the class has finished making their statements, have the other half give their statements about what they've just done and the class will guess where they've been.

EXAMPLE 2: STUDENT A: **Je viens de manger un sandwich.**
STUDENT B: **Tu viens du café?**
STUDENT A: **Non.**
STUDENT C: **Tu viens du restaurant?**
STUDENT A: **Oui, je viens du restaurant.**

UNITÉ 2   LE WEEKEND, ENFIN!

1. VOCABULAIRE: À LA CAMPAGNE   (Unit 2 Lesson 5 p. 100)

These activities target several intelligences: the **logical-mathematical** (making logical connections), **the spatial** (creating visuals), the **interpersonal** and **linguistic** (interacting in group conversations) and the **musical** (making animal sounds).

■ To Drill *Vocabulaire: À la campagne*

Go over the pronunciation of the vocabulary words on page 100. Then hand out one word to each student (see list of words on next page). Have each student say a word or words (in French or English) that one might associate with the target word. The class checks the vocabulary words on page 100 and guesses the word.

EXAMPLE: Target word: **une rivière**
          STUDENT: Mississippi, Nile, Amazon. . .
          CLASS: **Une rivière.**

You might do the first one as an example. Then have all students give their clues. When finished, repeat the words one at a time and ask the class to give you some of the clue words.

EXAMPLE: TEACHER: **une rivière.**
          CLASS: Mississippi, Amazon, Nile.

D.C. Heath and Company, a Division of Houghton Mifflin Company

VOCABULARY: À LA CAMPAGNE

1. une rivière
2. une forêt
3. un lac
4. un arbre
5. un poisson
6. une feuille
7. un écureuil
8. un oiseau
9. une ferme
10. un champ
11. une prairie
12. une plante
13. une vache
14. une fleur
15. un cochon
16. un lapin
17. un canard
18. une poule
19. un cheval
20. les endroits
21. les animaux

Have the class make sketches of the words you gave them. Supply them with colorful non-toxic markers and 8 1/2 x 11 white construction paper. Tell students to make large sketches of their vocabulary words on one side of the paper and to print the vocabulary word in large letters on the other side. Those that have words with irregular plurals **(animal, cheval, oiseau)** should write the singular and the plural of their words.

When all students have finished their visuals, collect them and show them to the class one at a time. Have the class give you the French word for the visual. After you have shown all the visuals once, show them again. This time ask the class to tell you if the picture is **un endroit** or **un animal**. You might divide the class into two groups, one group responding if the picture is **un endroit**, the other group responding if it is **un animal**. If the picture, such as **une plante**, **une fleur**, fits neither category, the class should respond with the word that defines the picture. Finally, select the animal visuals and drill them by activating your students' sound-loving intelligence. Divide the class into two groups. Show one group the animal pictures one at a time and have them make the animal sound. The other group then gives the French word. (Note that the second group should not be able to see the visuals.) You'll be surprised at how much fun students have making these animal sounds. Drill these words one last time, showing the words to the second group and having them make the animal sounds while the other group gives the French words.

Divide the class into groups of three or four. Give each student one of the visuals they just made. Have each student in the group make a statement about each visual.

EXAMPLE:	STUDENT A *shows visual and says:*	**C'est un cochon.**
	STUDENT B:	**Les cochons mangent beaucoup.**
	STUDENT C:	**Les cochons habitent dans une ferme.**
	STUDENT D:	**Les cochons sont gros.**

When all students have shown their pictures once and have gone through the above drill, have them either exchange pictures with another group and repeat this drill with new visuals or try a more advanced drill.

EXAMPLE: *Student A shows visual and each student in the group asks a question about the visual. Student A responds making up answers.*

Student A shows visual of **une vache.**

STUDENT B: **De quelle couleur est la vache?**
STUDENT A: **Elle est blanche et noire.**
STUDENT C: **Où est-ce que la vache habite?**
STUDENT A: **Elle habite dans une ferme.**
STUDENT D: **Est-ce que les vaches sont petites?**
STUDENT A: **Non, elles ne sont pas petites.**

When all visuals have been drilled, collect them and post them on the bulletin board with the title **À la campagne.**

2. LE PASSÉ COMPOSÉ AVEC *AVOIR*   (Unit 2 Lesson 6 pp. 104–105)

This activity targets the **linguistic** intelligence with a reading and writing activity. The **musical** intelligence is activated with classical background music which is to be played while students are reading.

■ To Drill *Le passé composé avec* avoir

Cover the material on pages 104–105 before doing this activity. Make copies of the worksheet on the next page. Give each student a worksheet, have them write their names on the papers and then fill in the blanks. Tell them that the entire class will be reading these papers. When all students have finished, have them pass their papers in such a way that all papers will pass through all hands and when students have their own papers back, they will have read all the papers.

Play some soft classical music during the reading period. Instruct students to read at their own pace and to try to remember what they've read since this information will be used in a game after the reading period. Students are not to take any notes. When a student finishes reading, he or she should pass the paper on to the next person. Some students may have to wait for papers to be passed on to them as there will be some slower readers. Ask them to sit back, relax, listen to the music and wait quietly. When students have their own papers back, that should signify that the papers have circulated through the entire class.

Now divide the class into two groups for the game. Collect the papers from Group 1. From these papers, Stack A, you will make questions to ask Group 2. Collect the papers from Group 2. From these papers, Stack B, you'll make questions to ask Group 1. Simply glance at a paper and ask a question about information on that paper: **«Qu'est-ce que Paul a mangé hier?»** or **«Qui a mangé une pomme hier?»** Note that Paul will not be in the group answering this question. Take one question from each paper and then put it on the bottom of the stack. This way you'll be asking questions about all students. Take turns asking one question to each group. Score one point for each correct answer.

Je m'appelle _____

Complete the following statements in French, describing things you have done this month.

1. **Ce mois j'ai visité** _____ *(town, city, place)*.

2. **Ce mois j'ai rendu visite à** _____ *(name of a person)*.

3. **Ce mois j'ai acheté** _____.

4. **Ce mois j'ai étudié** _____.

5. **Ce mois j'ai attendu** _____.

6. **Ce mois j'ai regardé** _____ *(a movie, a TV program)*.

Complete the following statements, describing things you did yesterday.

7. **Hier, j'ai parlé à** _____.

8. **Hier, j'ai écouté** _____.

9. **Hier, j'ai mangé** _____.

10. **Hier, j'ai fini (je n'ai pas fini)** _____.

3. QUELQUES PARTICIPES PASSÉS IRRÉGULIERS; *QUELQU'UN; NE... PERSONNE* (Unit 2 Lesson 7 pp. 117–118)

This activity targets the **bodily-kinesthetic**, **linguistic**, **interpersonal** and **intrapersonal** intelligences as students answer questions about themselves and then circulate trying to find classmates that will answer "yes" to these questions.

■ To Drill *eu, été, fait, mis, pris, vu; quelqu'un* and *ne... personne*

Before beginning this activity, go over the material on pages 117 and 118. Then write the questions (at the end of this activity) on the blackboard. Have students copy these questions and answer them in complete sentences. You might call on individuals to answer each question and write their answer on the board as an example. When all students have written their answers, have them stand and circulate, asking no more than two questions to each student. (After they have questioned all classmates, they may then go back and question someone again.) Students try to find "yes" answers to their questions. Once they find a "yes" answer, the student answering "yes" should sign his name next to the number of that question. When students have found a "yes" answer to all questions (or when they have questioned everyone) they may sit down. When you see that several students are seated, ask the rest of the class to be seated. Then begin asking the following type of questions.

TEACHER:	**Est-ce que quelqu'un a mis la table hier?** (Ask students to raise their hands if they found someone that set the table yesterday.)
STUDENT A:	**Oui, Mona a mis la table hier.**
STUDENT B:	**Justin a mis la table aussi.**

(Continue until you've called on all students who have raised their hands. Then go on to a second question.)

TEACHER:	**Est-ce que quelqu'un a fait ses devoirs hiers?**

When you come to a question for which no one has found a "yes" answer—no hands are raised—call on a few individual students. They should answer using **personne**.

STUDENT A: **Non. Personne n'a fait ses devoirs.**

QUESTIONS FOR ACTIVITY 3

1. Est-ce que tu as mis la table hier?
2. Est-ce que tu as fait tes devoirs hier?
3. Est-ce que tu as pris un taxi hier?
4. Est-ce que tu as mis une montre aujourd'hui?
5. Est-ce que tu as vu ton prof d'anglais aujourd'hui?
6. Est-ce que tu as fait des achats hier?
7. Est-ce que tu as eu la grippe hier?

4. LES VERBES COMME *SORTIR* ET *PARTIR*   (Unit 2 Lesson 8 p. 126)

This activity targets the **musical, linguistic** and **bodily-kinesthetic** intelligences as students sing and act out the conjugation of verbs.

■ To Drill *sortir, partir, dormir*

Before beginning this activity, cover the material on page 126. Then teach the song that follows, using the first half of the tune *Au clair de la lune.* If you are not musical, ask for a few volunteers to prepare and present the song. Have students act out the last line of the song to help them remember the meanings of the verbs. (If you are not familiar with this song, you can find it in *Savez-vous Planter les Choux? and other French Songs,* selected and illustrated by Anne Rockwell. World Publishing Company, Cleveland, 1969.)

> **... et ils dorment maintenant.** (Close eyes and lean head to side as if sleeping.)
>
> **...et ils partent maintenant.** (Wave hand as if saying goodbye.)
>
> **...et ils sortent maintenant.** (Make walking motion with first two fingers to indicate walking away or going out.)

Je Dors
(to the tune of Au Clair de la Lune)

1. *Je dors, tu dors, elle dort.*
   Nous dor-mons au-ssi.
   Vous dor-mez sou-vent et
   Ils dorment main-te-nant.

2. *Je pars, tu pars, elle part.*
   Nous par-tons au-ssi.
   Vous par-tez sou-vent et
   Ils partent main-te-nant.

3. *Je sors, tu sors, elle sort.*
   Nous sor-tons au-ssi.
   Vous sor-tez sou-vent et
   Ils sortent main-te-nant.

5. LES VERBES CONJUGUÉS AVEC *ÊTRE*   (Unit 2 Lesson 8 pp. 128–129)

This activity targets the **linguistic** and **bodily-kinesthetic** intelligences as students recite a story while their classmates act it out.

■ To Drill *Les verbes conjugués avec* être

Before beginning this activity, cover the material on pages 128–129. Then have students memorize the story on the next page to help them remember which verbs are conjugated with **être.** Assign each student a line to act out (if there are more or fewer than 16 students, you might give one student two lines or two students might act out one line). Go through the pronunciation and meaning of the story first. Then, the second time through, have students provide gestures or pantomime their lines as the entire group recites the story. The third time through the story, have the entire group recite the story and do the gestures or pantomime for each line. Finally, have students turn their papers face down and ask for a volunteer to try to recite the story relying on the other students to give the gestures as clues. The next day, have each student recite the story from memory with help from the class giving gestures. (Some students may prefer to write the story, glancing at the class for visual clues.)

UNE SEMAINE À PARIS

Je suis montée dans l'avion.

L'avion est parti.

Nous sommes arrivés à Paris.

Je suis descendue de l'avion.

Je suis partie en taxi.

Le taxi est passé par la Tour Eiffel.

Nous sommes arrivés à mon hôtel.

Je suis entrée dans ma chambre.

Je suis restée à Paris une semaine.

Je suis montée dans la Tour Eiffel.

Je suis allée au Louvre.

Je suis tombée dans la Seine.

Je suis devenue très pâle.

Je suis revenue à l'hôtel.

Ma mère est venue me voir.

Nous sommes rentrées aux États-Unis.

Unité 2°

UNITÉ 3   BON APPÉTIT!

1. LA NOURRITURE   (Unit 3 Lesson 9 pp. 146, 148, 150)

These activities target several intelligences: the **interpersonal** (group activity), the **spatial** and **intrapersonal** (drawing, self-expression), the **logical-mathematical** (categorizing foods), the **bodily-kinesthetic** (playing cards) and the **linguistic** (speaking).

■ To Drill *La nourriture*

After you have covered the material on pages 146, 148, and 150, review and drill the material with this activity. Give each student a copy of the list of foods on the next page. Then ask each student to name three foods and have the class guess the connection. Some connections may be obvious **(une poire, une fraise, une cerise—les fruits)**; others may be less obvious **(un café, la soupe, un thé—** hot foods). You might write some of the possible categories on the board: **les ingrédients, le poisson, la viande, les boissons, le dessert, les fruits, les légumes, la cuisine française,** foods that are cold, hot, round, foods in a sandwich, etc. Allow students to use some English in their explanation of categories if necessary.

Now divide your class into groups of four (one group of three or five if four doesn't work out). Give each group 56 index cards and some non-toxic color markers, crayons or colored pencils (if the markers show through the cards, use crayons or colored pencils). Each group is to draw and color sketches of the foods on the list, one drawing per card. At the bottom of each sketch, students should print the name of the food as it appears on the food list. Some students may do the drawing and then have other members of the group write the words or do the coloring. When all food visuals have been drawn, students are ready to begin playing the game. Hand out the game rules that follow to one student in each group. This student reads the rules to the group. Each student should have on hand their food list. Students may need to refer to their food list to figure out possible food categories.

FOOD LIST

1. une pomme
2. un croque-monsieur
3. un sandwich au saucisson
4. un yaourt nature
5. un yaourt à la fraise
6. un café
7. un chocolat
8. un thé glacé
9. un soda
10. un thé
11. une omelette nature
12. une omelette aux champignons
13. une pizza
14. une salade verte
15. une salade de tomates
16. une glace au chocolat
17. une glace à la vanille
18. une limonade
19. le lait
20. le pain
21. les céréales
22. la confiture
23. un oeuf
24. le thon
25. la sole
26. le saumon
27. les spaghetti
28. les frites
29. le riz
30. le jambon
31. le saucisson
32. la soupe
33. le fromage
34. le céleri
35. le gâteau
36. la tarte
37. le jus de pomme
38. le jus de raisin
39. un pamplemousse
40. une poire
41. une fraise
42. une cerise
43. une carotte
44. une pomme de terre
45. les petits pois
46. les haricots verts
47. le beurre
48. la margarine
49. le sel
50. le sucre
51. le poivre
52. le ketchup
53. la mayonnaise
54. la moutarde
55. le porc
56. une orange

GAME RULES

Number of players: three to five

Shuffle the cards and deal out seven cards to each player. Place the remaining cards in a stack face down (the draw pile). The dealer begins play by drawing a card (play and pass the deal in a clockwise direction). If he has any three cards that match (three fruits) or any three cards for which he can think of a connection (ham, mayonnaise, bread — foods for a sandwich), he lays them down face up and says what the connection or category is. If the group agrees with his reasoning, they say **Oui.** If the group does not agree, they say **Non** and the student must pick up the cards and put them back in his hand. However, if he thinks he is right, he may raise his hand and have the teacher come and give the final decision.

When a player lays down cards, he lays down sets of three. At the end of his turn, each player discards a card and places it face up in the discard pile. Players may draw up to four consecutive cards from the discard pile instead of drawing one from the draw pile. When the draw pile is gone, shuffle the discard pile and place it face down to use as the draw pile. Play ends when one player has no cards left in his hand. The winner of the game is the player with the most points. Count one point for each card laid down and subtract one point for each card in a player's hand. Record the scores. Then shuffle the cards and play the game again if time allows.

2. LE CHOIX DES ARTICLES (Unit 3 Lesson 11 pp. 168–170)

This activity targets several intelligences: the **linguistic** (speaking), the **spatial** (use of visuals), the **logical-mathematical** (categorizing), the **bodily-kinesthetic** (card game), and the **interpersonal** (group activity).

■ To Drill *Le choix des articles*

After you have covered the material on pages 168–170, divide your class into groups of four (three or five if need be). You should have the same number of groups as you did for Activity 1 because you will be using the decks of cards that students made for that activity.

The instructions are on the following page. Hand out instruction and category sheets to each student. Have them follow instructions to select the cards for the game and to play the game. Circulate to make sure each group is on task and is following the directions.

Before sending students to their groups, write the following dialog (to be used in the game) on the board and explain the use of the definite, indefinite or partitive article.

PLAYER A:	**As-tu des légumes, Paul?** (the food category must be mentioned first) *(Do you have some vegetables?)*
PAUL:	**Oui, j'ai des légumes.** (or **Non, je n'ai pas de légumes.**) *(Yes, I have <u>some vegetables</u>. or No, I don't have <u>any</u>.)*
PLAYER A:	**As-tu des haricots verts? (or As-tu une carotte?)** *(Do you have some green beans? or Do you have a carrot?)*
PAUL:	**Oui, j'ai des haricots verts.** *(Then, giving his card to Player A,)* **Voici les haricots verts.** *(Here are the green beans.)*

Player A continues asking for cards until he gets a negative response.

PLAYER A:	**As-tu des fruits, Marie?** *(Do you have <u>some</u> fruit?)*
MARIE:	**Non, je n'ai pas de fruits.** *(I don't have <u>any</u> fruit.)*

©D.C. Heath and Company, a Division of Houghton Mifflin Company.

INSTRUCTIONS FOR CARD GAME

Number of players: three to five

Shuffle and then deal out the entire deck of cards. Then, one at a time, place the cards that are listed on the category sheet under the proper category. Note that not all cards are used in this game. Each player selects the cards from his hand that appear on the category sheet and places them on the category sheet. Any remaining cards should be set aside as they will not be used in this card game.

Gather up all the cards on the category sheets. Each player will need to refer to the category sheets during the game in order to know what words are in each category. Shuffle your revised deck of cards and deal out six cards to each player. Place the remaining cards in a stack face down (the draw pile). Each player tries to get as many sets of three of a kind (three fruits, three meats, etc.) as he can.

The dealer starts by placing any sets of three that he has in his hand on the table. Then he asks another player for a kind of food that he already has in his hand. Example: Player has **les petits pois** so he can ask for vegetables. He cannot ask for a type of food that he does not have in hand unless he is out of cards. Players must listen to find out who has what. The following dialog is an example of questions and answers you might use.

PLAYER A:	**As-tu des légumes, Paul?** *(the food category must be mentioned first)*
PAUL:	**Oui, j'ai des légumes.**
PLAYER A:	**As-tu des haricots verts?** *(une carotte?)*
PAUL:	**Oui, j'ai des haricots verts.** *(Giving his card to Player A)* **Voici les haricots verts.**

Player A continues asking for cards until he gets a negative response.

PLAYER A:	**As-tu des fruits, Marie?**
MARIE:	**Non, je n'ai pas de fruits.**

When a player gets a negative response, he lays down any sets of three from his hand and draws a card from the draw pile. (Play continues even when the draw pile is gone.) The next player takes his turn (playing in a clockwise direction). Play continues until all cards are laid down. The winner is the one with the most points. Count one point for each card laid down. Keep a running total of each player's score. Play several hands. The player with the highest score when the time is up wins.

CATEGORY SHEET FOR ACTIVITY 2

LES FRUITS

un pamplemousse
une poire
une fraise
une cerise
une pomme
une orange

LES LÉGUMES

les petits pois
les haricots verts
une pomme de terre
une carotte
une salade verte
une salade de tomates
le céleri

LES INGRÉDIENTS

le beurre
la margarine
le sel
le sucre
le poivre
la mayonnaise
la moutarde

LES DESSERTS

une glace au chocolat
la tarte
le gâteau
une glace à la vanille
un yaourt nature
un yaourt à la fraise

LA VIANDE

le jambon
le saucisson
le porc

LE POISSON

le thon
la sole
le saumon

LES BOISSONS

le lait
le jus de pomme
le jus de raisin
un soda
un thé glacé
un café
une limonade
un chocolat

© D.C. Heath and Company, a Division of Houghton Mifflin Company.

3. L'ADJECTIF *TOUT*   (Unit 3 Lesson 12 pp. 180)

This activity targets the **musical** and **linguistic** intelligences as students sing a song to drill the use of the different forms of **tout**. The **spatial** intelligence is also activated as students receive visual cues for parts of the song.

■ To Drill *L'adjectif* tout

Before beginning this drill, go over the material on page 180. Then make four visuals: **tous les choux** (draw several cabbages on one side of a sheet of construction paper and write **tous les choux** on the other side); **toutes les fraises** (draw several strawberries on one side of the visual and write the phrase **toutes les fraises** on the other side); **tout le pain** (draw a loaf of French bread on one side of visual and write **tout le pain** on the other side); **toute la tarte** (draw a pie on one side of the visual and write **toute la tarte** on the other side).

Practice drilling the visuals with the class, showing them the picture and having them give you the correct phrase. When they can easily give you the correct response, they are ready to learn the song.

Hand out the words to the song (see next page). If you are musical, sing the song for the the class. Then have everyone sing the song together a few times. (If you are not musical, have some students volunteer to teach the song to the class. If you need the music, you might get the following book from your local library: *Savez-vous Planter les Choux? and Other French Songs,* selected and illustrated by Anne Rockwell, World Publishing, Cleveland, 1969.) Once the class has learned the song, divide the class into Group A and Group B. Next, have them sing the song through with one group asking the questions and one group answering. Give four students the visuals and tell them to hold them up when they hear the corresponding words. Sing the song through as it is written a few times. Finally, tell the class that you will show them visuals of the foods at random and they should sing about the visual you are holding up.

EXAMPLE: You show **la tarte**. Group A sings: **Avez-vous mangé la tarte? Toute la tarte? Toute la tarte?,** etc. Groups B responds.

Unité 3

Avez-vouz mangé les choux?

(to the tune of *Savez-vous planter les choux?*)

1. **Group A:** *Avez-vous man-gé les choux, tous les choux, tous les choux?*

   Group B: *Nous avons man-gé les choux, tous les choux, tous les choux.*

2. **Group A:** *Avez-vous man-gé les fraises, toutes les fraises, toutes les fraises?*

   Group B: *Nous avons man-gé les fraises, toutes les fraises, toutes les fraises.*

3. **Group A:** *Avez-vous man-gé le pain, tout le pain, tout le pain?*

   Group B: *Nous avons man-gé le pain, tout le pain, tout le pain.*

4. **Group A:** *Avez-vous man-gé la tarte, toute le tarte, toute le tarte?*

   Group B: *Nous avons man-gé la tarte, toute le tarte, toute le tarte.*

UNITÉ 4   LES LOISIRS ET LES SPECTACLES

1. LES SPECTACLES; AU CINÉMA   (Unit 4 Lesson 13 pp.194, 196)

This activity targets the **linguistic** intelligence through the use of language. The **logical-mathematical** intelligence is activated as students think of words associated with the target words. Other students are challenged to make the connection between the clue words and the target word.

■ To Drill Vocabulary: *Les spectacles; Au cinéma*

After you have introduced the material on pages 194 and 196, give one of the vocabulary words from the next page to each student. Have each student think of an example of the word. The student gives a clue and the class tries to guess the target word. If the class does not guess the word, have the student give a second clue.

EXAMPLE: *Student has* **un acteur** *and says, "Tom Cruise."*
CLASS RESPONDS: **Un acteur.**

EXAMPLE: *Student has* **une chanteuse** *and says, "Gloria Estefan."*
CLASS RESPONDS: **Une joueuse.**
STUDENT: **Non.** *(Then gives another clue.)* Barbra Streisand.
CLASS: **Une chanteuse.**

Allow students to have their books open and scan the possible vocabulary during this activity. Once all students have given their clues, collect the target words and read them to the class one at a time. This time ask the class to give you the clue they heard previously for the target word.

EXAMPLE: TEACHER: **Un acteur.**
CLASS: Tom Cruise.
TEACHER: **Une chanteuse.**
CLASS: Gloria Estefan, Barbra Streisand.

LIST OF WORDS FOR ACTIVITY 1

Make a copy of this list, then cut out words, giving one or more to each student. If
you have more students than words on the list, make a second copy of the list. More
than one student can have the same word.

1. un film

2. un acteur

3. une actrice

4. une pièce de théâtre

5. un orchestre

6. un groupe

7. un chanteur

8. une chanteuse

9. une chanson

10. une exposition

11. un match

12. une équipe

13. un joueur

14. une joueuse

15. un film d'aventures

16. un film policier

17. un film d'horreur

18. un film de science-fiction

19. un drame psychologique

20. un dessin animé

21. une comédie

22. une comédie musicale

2. VOCABULAIRE: RAPPORTS ET SERVICES PERSONNELS
(Unit 4 Lesson 14 p. 205)

This activity targets the **intrapersonal** intelligence as students write about themselves. The **linguistic** intelligence is also targeted as students read, write and respond to questions. The **musical** intelligence is activated by playing soft background music during the silent reading activity.

■ To Drill: *présenter…à, apporter…à, donner…à, montrer. . .à, prêter…à, rendre…à.*

Before beginning this drill, introduce the vocabulary on page 205. Then make copies of the student handout on the next page. Give one to each student and allow the class time to fill in the blanks. (Suggested answers are given, but students may fill in original answers.) Tell them that this information is going to be read by the rest of the class. Ask if anyone has a question about the meanings of the sentences. When everyone has finished, have students pass their paper to another student (arrange an order of passing papers so that the papers will circulate the room and when students receive their own paper back they will have read all papers). Be sure students have their names on their papers.

Students should read at their own pace and not be hurried; they should try to remember as much as they can about what they read. When a student has finished reading a paper he passes it on to the next person and then he should quietly wait until he receives a paper. Encourage students to relax and not rush the slower readers. Play some soft background music during the reading activity.

When all students have finished reading, collect the papers and scan them. Make up some questions to ask the class. Be sure to ask at least one question for each paper.

<table>
<tr><td>EXAMPLE:</td><td>TEACHER:</td><td>**Qui a presenté son copain à ses parents?**</td></tr>
<tr><td></td><td>STUDENT:</td><td>**Paul a presenté son copain à ses parents.**</td></tr>
<tr><td></td><td>TEACHER:</td><td>**Qu'est-ce que Marie a apporté à l'école?**</td></tr>
<tr><td></td><td>STUDENT:</td><td>**Elle a apporté un sandwich.**</td></tr>
</table>

Unité 4

Je m'appelle _____

Write about some things you have done by filling in the blanks with appropriate words. Some examples are given to help you understand the meanings of the sentences.

1. J'ai presenté _____ à mes parents.
    (mon prof, John, mon copain)

2. J'ai apporté _____ à l'école.
    (une radio, un sandwich)

3. J'ai donné _____ à mon/ma _____.
    (une montre, une chemise)   (cousin, frère, soeur, mère)

4. J'ai montré _____ à mes amis.
    (une photo, mon chien, ma voiture)

5. J'ai prêté _____ à quelqu'un.
    (un livre, mes devoirs?!)

6. J'ai rendu _____ à _____.
    (le dictionnaire, le livre)   (ma soeur, mon prof)

3. LES PRONOMS COMPLÉMENTS *LE, LA, LES*

(Unit 4 Lesson 15 pp. 216–217)

This activity targets the **musical** and **linguistic** intelligences as students learn a song which helps them understand the use of the direct object pronouns.

■ To Drill *Les pronoms compléments* le, la, les

Before beginning this drill, introduce the material on pages 216 and 217. Then introduce the song on the following page, which is set to the tune of the French folksong, *Sur le Pont d'Avignon.* (If you are not musical, have some students volunteer to teach the song to the class. If you need the music, you might get the following book from your local library: *Savez-vous Planter les Choux? and Other French Songs,* selected and illustrated by Anne Rockwell, World Publishing, Cleveland, 1969.) Divide your class into two groups, one group will be asking the question, the other group will be answering. The names in the song are to be replaced with the names of your students. You walk around the class pointing out a student or students. The class puts that name or names into the song. Repeat the song several times using different names each time.

Unité 4

Invitons-la!
(to the tune of *Sur le Pont d'Avignon*)

VERSE 1

Group 1:   A-vez-vous fait la con-nais-sance de notre a-mie, Ma-ry?

Group 2:   Nous a-vons fait la con-nais-sance de votre a-mie, Ma-ry.

Group 1:   In-vi-tons-la! Oui, oui.

Group 2:   In-vi-tons-la! Oui, oui.

VERSE 2

Group 1:   A-vez-vous fait la con-nais-sance de notre a-mi, Bar-ry?

Group 2:   Nous a-vons fait la con-nais-sance de votre a-mi, Bar-ry.

Group 1:   In-vi-tons-la! Oui, oui.

Group 2:   In-vi-tons-la! Oui, oui.

VERSE 3

Group 1:   A-vez-vous fait la con-nais-sance de nos a-mis, Paul et Jacques?

Group 2:   Nous a-vons fait la con-nais-sance de vos a-mis, Paul et Jacques.

Group 1:   In-vi-tons-les! Oui, oui.

Group 2:   In-vi-tons-les! Oui, oui.

4. VOCABULAIRE: *ON LIT, ON ÉCRIT, ON DIT*

(Unit 4 Lesson 15 p.225)

> This activity targets the **spatial** and **bodily-kinesthetic** intelligences as students put together collages. The **interpersonal** intelligence is also targeted as students work in groups. The **linguistic** intelligence is activated through an oral drill.

■ To Drill *Vocabulaire: on lit, on écrit, on dit*

Before beginning this activity, introduce the material on page 225. Then divide the class into groups of three or four and assign each group one of the vocabulary categories on that page. (If you have more than three groups, some will be working with the same vocabulary.) The group that has **On lit...** will need to find the items or pictures of the items listed: **un journal, un magazine, un roman, des bandes dessinées, une histoire, une revue.** The group that has **On écrit...** will need to look for the following: **un journal** *(diary),* **une carte, un poème, une carte postale, une lettre.** The group that has **On dit...** will find pictures that represent **un mensonge** and **la vérité.** This last group will have the more difficult assignment. You might suggest they look for false advertising. They might use a picture of George Washington to represent truth and a picture of Pinochio with a long nose to represent a lie.

   Give each group ten minutes to figure out what they are going to put on their collage and to decide who is going to look for the different items. Tell them to bring the items to class the next day and they will then have class time to put the collage together.

   The next day, bring magazines to class that the students can use to cut out pictures. (I often find many students forget to bring their materials.) If students can't find the appropriate pictures for each vocabulary word, allow them to draw a sketch on their collage. Give each group a large sheet of tagboard for the collage. Each group will also need the following: scissors, non-toxic glue, one dark non-toxic marker and a few sheets of white construction paper.

Unité 4

When each group has assembled their pictures they should arrange them in categories on the collage.

EXAMPLE:

Put all the comics in one section, the newspapers in another, etc. The collage **On lit...** would have five different sections: **une revue/un magazine, des bandes dessinées, une histoire, un roman, un journal.** This group would use **On lit...** for the title of their collage. They should also label each group of pictures with corresponding vocabulary words. Have students write the vocabulary words on small strips of white construction paper and glue these on to the collage.

When all students have finished their collages, have one person from each group come to the front of the class one at a time and hold up the collage for all to see. You then ask the class questions about each collage. For the collage(s) entitled **On lit...** , ask the following questions:

TEACHER:	*(pointing to a picture of a magazine)* **Qu'est-ce qu'on lit?**
CLASS:	**On lit une revue/une magazine.**
TEACHER:	*(Pointing to a comic strip)* **Qu'est-ce qu'on lit?**
CLASS:	**On lit des bandes dessinées.**

Continue asking this type of question until all the vocabulary words on the collage have been drilled. Then have the student holding up the collage turn it away from the students so that only you can see the pictures. Now, one at a time, say a vocabulary word that is on the collage and ask the class for a specific example taken from the collage.

| EXAMPLE: | TEACHER: | **un journal.** |
| | CLASS: | *The Star Herald.* |

To drill the collage entitled **On écrit...,** point to different things on the collage and call on individual students to make a statement: **On écrit <u>une lettre</u>.**

To drill the collage entitled **On dit...,** ask the questions: **Qui dit la vérité?** and **Qui dit un mensonge?** Students respond with the name of the person pictured.

©D. C. Heath and Company, a Division of Houghton Mifflin Company

Cut the **On dit...** collage into two sections: **un mensonge** and **la vérité.** Have two students each hold one section of the collage and stand at the front of the room at opposite sides. Tell the class that you are going to make some statements. The class is to listen to the statements and decide if they are true or false. They then give a gesture to indicate true or false. If the statement is true, students extend their arm to the left or right, whichever side of the room contains **la vérité** collage. The student holding **la vérité** collage should then raise it high.

TEACHER:	**Je dis qu'il fait beau.** *(Students respond with a gesture and teacher calls on one individual.)*
STUDENT A:	**On dit la vérité.** (or **Vous dites la vérité.**)
TEACHER:	**Je dis que Mark est blond.** *(Students respond with a gesture. Teacher calls on individual student.)*
STUDENT:	**On dit un mensonge.** (or **Vous dites un mensonge.**)

Finally, ask for some volunteers to make some statements, true or false. Remind students that they should not be saying anything negative about teachers or students.

| STUDENT C: | **Je dis que je suis américain.** *(Students give a gesture indicating true or false. Student C calls on another student.)* |
| STUDENT D: | **Tu dis la vérité.** (or **Tu dis un mensonge.**) |

Continue this drill until several students have given statements. Post the collages in your room to reinforce this vocabulary visually.

UNITÉ 5 LES SPORTS ET LA VIE QUOTIDIENNE

1. LES PARTIES DU CORPS (Unit 5 Lesson 17 p. 258)

> This activity targets the **bodily, musical** and **linguistic** intelligences as students act out a song about parts of the body.

■ To Drill *Les parties du corps*

Before beginning this activity, cover the material on page 258 of the Student Text.

Je lève le bras gauche

Je lève le bras gauche. Moi aussi, je lève le bras gauche.

Je lève le bras droit. Moi aussi, je lève le bras droit.

Je plie les– jambes. Moi aussi, je plie les jambes.

Je touche le pied gauche. Mon aussi, je touche le pied gauche.
Je touche la jambe droite. Mon aussi, je touche la jambe droite.
Je touche l'oreille gauche. Mon aussi, je touche l'oreille gauche.
Je touche le dos. Mon aussi, je touche le dos.

Stand in a circle and act out the song as you sing it. Begin leading the song with students repeating. The second time, let students make up lines that the rest of the class repeats.

2. LA SANTÉ   (Unit 5 Lesson 17 pp. 260–261)

This activity targets the **linguistic** and **bodily-kinesthetic** intelligences as students act out charade sentences.

■ To Drill *La santé*

Hand out a charade sentence to each student to act out one at a time as the class guesses the sentence. When all sentences have been presented, ask each student to say his or her sentence and call on a classmate to give the gestures. If the classmate is having trouble remembering, the rest of the class should help out by giving some gestures.

CHARADE SENTENCES

1. Je suis en forme.

2. Je suis malade.

3. Il a la grippe.

4. Nous avons un rhume.

5. Ils sont fatigués.

6. J'ai mal à la tête.

7. Elle a mal au dos.

8. Il a mal aux oreilles.

9. J'ai mal au ventre.

10. Vous avez mal aux yeux.

11. Nous avons mal aux pieds.

12. Il a mal à l'épaule.

13. Elle a mal aux dents.

14. Tu as mal à la jambe.

15. Nous avons mal aux genoux.

16. Je suis en bonne santé.

17. Je me sens bien.

18. Je suis en mauvaise santé.

19. Je ne me sens pas bien.

20. Elle a la gripe.

21. Vous avez un rhume.

3. VOCABULAIRE: POUR EXPRIMER SON OPINION
(Unit 5 Lesson 18 p. 269)

This activity targets the **intrapersonal** intelligence as students are asked to give their opinion about various things (objects, movies, music). The **spatial** and **bodily-kinesthetic** intelligences are activated as students look at objects and pass them around the room. The **musical** intelligence is activated as students listen to music.

■ To Drill *à mon avis, selon moi, d'après moi, je pense que, je trouve que, je crois que*

Before you begin this drill, cover the material on page 269. Bring to class some of the materials listed below.

1. a painting or a large picture of a painting
2. a hat
3. a ring with a price tag on it
4. a photo of a middle-aged woman
5. music tapes—play three different kinds of music. Give students time to write an opinion for each.
6. the name of a popular movie

Hand out the student worksheet that follows for students to use for their answers. Show the class a painting. Pass it around the class if possible. Have students write their opinion of the painting by filling in #1 on the worksheet. Provide them with additional adjectives if need be. Call on a few individuals for an oral response. You might use this phrase: **Qu'est-ce que tu penses de la peinture?** Students should respond using the phrase on their paper: **À mon avis, la peinture est belle.** Then continue with #2. Show students the hat. Pass it around the room or walk around the room modeling it. Have students write their opinions of the hat.

Once again, ask a few students their opinion of the object. This time they will respond using the phrase **selon moi.** Continue presenting the rest of the objects in like manner.

Unité 5

When students have finished, collect the papers and hand them out, making sure students don't get their own paper. Then write the conjugation of **croire** on the board. Ask students questions using the verb **croire.** Follow the structured dialog:

TEACHER:	**Qui croit que la peinture est belle?**
STUDENT A *(who has Jack's paper):*	**Jack croit que la peinture est belle.**
TEACHER:	**Qui croit que la peinture est superbe?**
STUDENT B:	**Marie croit que la peinture est superbe.**
STUDENT C:	**Paul croit que la peinture est superbe.**
TEACHER:	**Qu'est-ce que vous croyez, Paul et Marie?**
PAUL ET MARIE:	**Nous croyons que la peinture est superbe.**
TEACHER *(asking the class):*	**Qu'est-ce qu'ils croient?**
CLASS:	**Ils croient que la peinture est superbe.**

Continue asking questions about opinions on the other subjects.

Je m'appelle _____

Express your opinion by filling in the blanks with one of the suggested adjectives or with an original adjective.

1. À mon avis, la peinture est _____ (superbe, belle, laide, moderne, intéressante).

2. Selon moi, le chapeau est _____ (élégant, joli, ridicule, démodé, à la mode).

3. D'après moi, la bague est _____ (bon marché, chère, trop chère).

4. Je pense que la femme a _____ ans *(write a number)*.

5. (a) Je trouve que cette musique est _____ (bonne, mauvaise, superbe, ennuyeuse).

    (b) Je trouve que cette musique est _____.

    (c) Je trouve que cette musique est _____.

6. Je crois que ce film est _____ (amusant, étrange, intéressant, ennuyeux, bon, mauvais).

Unité 5

4. LES VERBES RÉFLÉCHIS; LA TOILETTE (Unit 5 Lesson 19 p. 275–279)

These activities activate the **spatial** and **bodily-kinesthetic** intelligences as students draw visuals of vocabulary words and also act out these words. The **linguistic** and **interpersonal** intelligences are targeted in a group activity in which students create sentences for each visual.

■ To Drill *Les verbes réfléchis; les articles de toilette*

Before beginning these activities, cover the material on pages 275–279. Then assign a vocabulary word to each student. Provide students with light-colored construction paper (8 1/2 x 11) and non-toxic colored markers. Instruct students to draw the vocabulary word on one side of the paper and to print it in large letters on the other side.

VOCABULARY WORDS

VERBS

se réveiller, se lever, s'habiller, se promener, se reposer, se coucher, se laver (les cheveux), se brosser (les dents), se maquiller, se peigner, se raser

NOUNS

une brosse à dents, un peigne, une brosse à cheveux, du shampooing, du rouge à lèvres, du dentifrice, du savon, un rasoir

---

When all students have finished their visuals, collect them and show the sketches to the class. Ask them to guess which vocabulary word is represented in the sketch. When you have gone through all the visuals in this manner, divide the class into two groups. Show Group A the word side of the visuals and ask them to act out the word. Group B should not be able to see the words but will guess the words by watching the gestures. After you have covered all the visuals in this manner, have the groups switch roles. This time show Group B the words and they will act them out. Group A will respond with the vocabulary words.

For this next activity you will need only these visuals: **une brosse à dents, un peigne, une brosse à cheveux, du shampooing, du rouge à lèvres, du dentifrice, du savon, un rasoir, se laver (les cheveux), se brosser (les dents), se maquiller, se peigner, se raser.**

Hand out these visuals to the students at random. Not all students will have a visual unless you have a small class. Name a verb and a subject and the student that has that verb and subject responds by conjugating the verb. Then the student that has an object that has a "connection" to that verb reponds by finishing the sentence. Follow this dialog:

TEACHER:	to put on make-up, she
STUDENT A *(holding up visual):*	**Elle se maquille.**
STUDENT B *(holding up visual):*	**Elle se maquille avec du rouge à lèvres.**

If Student A or Student B do not respond, the class can help out by chanting the response: **Elle se maquille, elle se maquille...** or **du rouge à lèvres, du rouge à lèvres.** Involve other students also by asking questions about the statement that has been made.

TEACHER:	**Qui se maquille?**
STUDENT C:	**Elle se maquille.**
TEACHER:	**Est-ce qu'elle se maquille avec une brosse à dents?**
STUDENT D:	**Non, elle se maquille avec du rouge à lèvres.**

Make a point of calling on students who are not holding visuals so all participate. After you have covered all visuals in this way, collect them.

For this last activity, you will need only the eleven verb visuals made from the first activity. Divide the class into four groups (or two groups if your class size is 12 or less). Hand out the pictures so that each group has about the same number. Each group should have a group leader who holds up one visual at a time. Each group member is then asked to make up one sentence about the picture. Each time a sentence is made a different subject should be used. When all group members have contributed a sentence, the group leader holds up a different visual and the drill continues as before. Students must make a sentence that contains more than just the subject and verb.

Unité 5

EXAMPLE:	*Group Leader shows* **se brosser (les dents)**
STUDENT A:	**Je me brosse les dents avec Crest.**
STUDENT B:	**Vous vous brossez les dents après le diner.**
STUDENT C:	**Tu te brosses les dents souvent.**
STUDENT D:	**Ils ne se brossent pas les dents.**

When each group has finished with their visuals, have them exchange with another group and continue drilling the verbs. Continue this activity until all groups have had a chance to drill all visuals.

5. QUELQUES VERBES RÉFLÉCHIS (Unit 5 Lesson 20 pp. 284–285)

This activity targets the **logical-mathematical** and **linguistic** intelligences as students give "clue" words that one might associate with the target vocabulary.

■ To Drill *s'amuser, s'arrêter, se dépêcher, s'excuser, se souvenir (de), se reposer, se taire, s'asseoir*

Before beginning this drill, cover the material on pages 284–285. Then write the vocabulary words listed above with their meanings on the blackboard. Pronounce these words for the class. Then give students slips of paper containing a word from the list. Ask them to make up some clue words that might be associated with their word.

> EXAMPLE: target word **s'amuser**
> clue words: **mes amis, une fête, mon anniversaire.**
> Class guesses: **s'amuser.**

Students give clues and the rest of the class guesses the word. After all clues have been given, ask each student to say his or her vocabulary word. Ask the class to give the clue words that they already heard for that word.

> EXAMPLE: Student says: **une fête, mes amis, mon anniversaire.**
> Class responds: **s'amuser**

Unité 5

UNITÉ 6 CHEZ NOUS

1. LE MOBILIER ET L'ÉQUIPEMENT DE LA MAISON

(Unité 6, Lesson 21 pp. 302-303)

This activity targets the **spatial** intelligence as students draw furniture. The **linguistic** intelligence is challenged as students respond to questions about the furniture.

■ To Drill *Le mobilier et l'équipement de la maison*

Before beginning this activity, cover the material on pages 302–303. Provide students with a large (12 x 18) white sheet of construction paper. Instruct them to draw and label the following rooms: **le living, la salle à manger, la cuisine, une chambre, la salle de bains.** The rooms should be large and might be on both sides of the paper. Have them draw furniture (again large) in the rooms using vocabulary from pages 302–303. When they have finished, go over the drills below, which should be on the board. Then pair them up and have them begin the drills. If you have an uneven number of students, you will need to do a drawing so you can be a partner.

Student A, showing drawing to partner, asks where some furniture is. The partner points to the objects mentioned and tells what room they are in.

STUDENT A:	**Où est le sofa?**
STUDENT B:	**Le sofa est dans le living.**
STUDENT A:	**Où est le lavabo?**
STUDENT B:	**Le lavabo est dans la salle de bains.**

Student A continues asking five or six questions about the location of furniture and Student B responds. Students switch roles and repeat this exercise.

Then Student B shows his drawing to Student A. Student A has a minute to study the drawing and then returns it to Student B. Student B now asks Student A to name all of the furniture in two of the rooms.

STUDENT B: **Qu'est-ce qu'il y a dans la salle à manger?**

STUDENT A: **Dans la salle à manger il y a quatre chaises et une table.**

STUDENT B: **Qu'est-ce qu'il y a dans la salle de bains?**

STUDENT A: **Dans la salle de bains, il y a une douche, un lavabo...**

(If Student A doesn't remember everything, Student B can give clues in French or English.) Students switch roles and repeat this exercise a second time.

Collect all drawings and hand them out at random, making sure that no one has his or her own drawing. Now begin asking questions.

TEACHER: **Qui a un lave-vaisselle?**

Students raise hands if the drawing they have has the furniture mentioned.

STUDENT A: **Dans la cuisine de Kathy, il y a un lave-vaisselle.**

STUDENT B: **Dans la cuisine de Paul, il y a un lave-vaisselle.**

Teacher continues a variety of questions to drill the vocabulary.

TEACHER: **Qui a une baignoire et une douche?**
Combien de chaises est-ce qu'il y a dans la salle à manger de Pierre?
Est-ce qu'il y a un tapis dans la cuisine de Marie?

2. LES PRONOMS RELATIFS *QUI* ET *QUE*

(Unit 6, Lesson 22, pp. 310–312)

This activity targets several intelligences: the **logical-mathematical** and **linguistic** (creating sentences), the **bodily-kinesthetic** (using manipulatives) and the **interpersonal** (group activity). The **musical** intelligence is activated as background music is played during the group activity.

■ To Drill *Les pronoms relatifs **qui** et **que***

Before beginning this activity, cover the material on pages 310–312. Make copies of the student worksheet (one per group of three students) and of the word list; cut up the words and put them into an envelope. You will need one envelope with a set of words for each group of students. Divide your class into groups of three, trying to have at least one student in each group that has a good understanding of the grammar. Instruct the groups to create as many sentences as possible. Each sentence should make sense and be grammatically correct. Each sentence should also contain one of the relative pronouns. Instruct students to take the words out of the envelopes and organize them in the categories listed on the student worksheet. Then have them begin manipulating the words in order to make sentences. Instruct one student (who has good handwriting) to write down the sentences that are created. Play some soft background music while students are creating sentences. Give the class about fifteen minutes, then have each group exchange their work with another group. Their task now is to scan the sentences, circling mistakes and correcting the errors if possible. When finished, each group should count the number of correct sentences and put that number at the top of the page. Collect the papers and announce the group that had the most correct sentences. Then return papers to each group so they can see what errors they made.

Je m'appelle _____

Je m'appelle _____

Je m'appelle _____

Arrange the words you receive in the following categories. This will help you create your sentences more quickly. Then create as many sentences as you can by manipulating the words. Each sentence should make sense and must contain one of the relative pronouns **qui** or **que**. One student in your group is to write down the list of sentences you create. Later, another group will be reading and correcting your sentences.

Pronouns or nouns	Relative pronouns	Verbs	"Leftovers" (miscellaneous words)
_____	_____	_____	_____
_____	_____	_____	_____
_____	_____	_____	_____
_____	_____	_____	_____
_____	_____	_____	_____
_____	_____	_____	_____
_____	_____	_____	_____

JE	J'	QUI
QUE	DANS	HABITE
NEW YORK	À	AI
UN	UNE	COPAIN
PARLE	LE	EST
PROFESSEUR	ITALIEN	MAISON
CONNAIS	VOICI	BLANCHE
VAIS ACHETER	ADMIRE	LA

Some possible sentences for Activity 2:

1. J'ai un copain qui habite à New York.
2. J'ai un copain qui habite dans une maison blanche.
3. J'ai un copain qui parle italien.
4. J'ai un copain qui est italien.
5. Je connais un professeur qui est italien.
6. J'ai un copain que j'admire.
7. J'ai un professeur que j'admire.
8. Voici la maison que je vais acheter.
9. Voici la masion blanche que je vais acheter.
10. Voici le professeur que j'admire.
11. Voici le professeur qui habite dans une maison blanche.
12. Voici le professeur qui habite à New York.
13. Voici le professeur italien que j'admire.
14. Je connais un professeur italien qui habite à New York.

3. L'USAGE DE L'IMPARFAIT: ÉVÉNEMENTS HABITUELS
(Unit 6, Lesson 23 pp. 319–321)

This activity targets the **intrapersonal** intelligence as students write about themselves. The **linguistic** intelligence is targeted through reading, writing, speaking and listening. The **bodily-kinesthetic** intelligence is activated as students pass papers.

■ To Drill *L'usage de l'imparfait: événements habituels*

Before beginning this activity, cover the material on pages 319–321. Assign students Exercise 5 on page 319, telling them to write out complete sentences. Let them know that the rest of the class will be reading their papers. You might participate by writing out this exercise so students can read about your childhood. Have students write their names on the papers and pass them around so that everyone reads all the papers. (You may need to have a couple of students carry papers between rows.) Students are to read each paper and are not to pass the papers until you say «**Passez les papiers.**» Each time papers are passed, give students time to read and then begin asking questions. Ask two or three questions and then say: «**Passez les papiers.**»

Continue this activity until papers have circulated the room. Possible questions: (You might write these questions on the board as you ask them.)

TEACHER: **Où habitait la famille de Mark (Sue, Amber)?**

STUDENT *(who has Mark's paper responds):* **Sa famille habitait à la campagne.**

TEACHER: **Qui habitait dans le centre-ville?**

Students who have the papers of other students who lived in **"le centre-ville"** *raise their hands and respond:*

Sue et sa famille habitaient dans le centre-ville (or La famille de Sue habitait dans le centre-ville.)

TEACHER: **Qui allait à l'école en bus (à pied, à vélo)? Qu'est-ce que Paul collectionnait? Qui se couchait à neuf heures? Qui voulait être actrice? Qu'est-ce que Monique voulait être?**

Continue asking a variety of questions until the papers have passed through all hands. Then collect the papers. Scan them quickly and select one that has some interesting answers. Now tell the class that you're going to see if they can remember how this student completed his sentences. The individual whose paper you're reading may not respond. Begin reading the sentences and have the class as a group fill in the reponses.

TEACHER:	This is Mary's paper.
	Ma famille et moi, nous habitions...
CLASS:	**dans la banlieue.**

(Most often someone in the class will remember the correct answer. Mary is to respond **«Oui»** or **«Non.»** If her response is **«Non»** she then gives the correct answer.) Next, select a few papers and read four or five sentences and challenge the class to guess whose paper you are reading.

EXAMPLE:	**Mon acteur favori était Tom Cruise.**
	Je collectionnais les timbres.
	Je voulais être pilote.
	À la télé, je regardais surtout les sports.

UNITÉ 7   SOYEZ À LA MODE!

1. LES TISSUS ET LES AUTRES MATIÈRES (Unit 7 Lesson 25 p. 349)

This activity targets the **bodily-kinesthetic** intelligence as students are challenged to identify materials through their sense of touch. The **linguistic** intelligence is activated as students write down the target vocabulary words. The **spatial** intelligence is activated when students finally see the materials.

■ To Drill *Les tissus et les autres matières*

Before beginning this activity, cover the material on pages 349–350. You will need the following materials for this activity:

- small paper bags (one for each of the materials you bring)
- small swatches of some of these fabrics: **le coton, le nylon, le polyester, le velours, le velours côtelé, la laine, la toile, la soie.**
- Some of these materials: **l'argent, l'or, le cuir, le caoutchouc, le plastique, la fourrure.**

(Do not use any objects, such as a silver knife or fork, that would prick a student who reaches in the bag to feel the object.)

Number the bags with a marker. Tell students to write numbers on their papers to total the number of bags being used. Pass the bags around the room and have each student reach in to feel the object without looking. The student then writes down what he or she thinks the object is. If a student is looking in bag #3, he or she writes the answer down for #3. (Allow students to check the vocabulary in the book on page 349.)

When all students have had a chance to feel all the materials, go over the answers with the group. When you receive the correct answer for what is in bag #1, take the material out and show the class. Continue in like manner until you have taken the materials out of all the bags.

When you show the materials you might ask further questions, such as: **«De quelle couleur est le coton?»**

2. LA DESCRIPTION DES VÊTEMENTS (Unit 7 Lesson 25 p. 349)

This activity targets the **spatial** and **bodily-kinesthetic** intelligences as students make collages using different patterns of fabrics and other materials. The **interpersonal** intelligence is activated with a group activity.

■ To Drill *La description des vêtements*

Before beginning this activity, cover the material on page 349. Then have students make small collages which you can use as flash cards to drill the new vocabulary. Allow students to work alone or with a partner. Discuss this project with the class a day or two ahead so they can bring materials from home. Have students choose the theme of their collage from these vocabulary words: shades of blue **(bleu, bleu clair, bleu foncé), le tissu uni, le tissu à rayures, le tissu à carreaux, le tissu à fleurs, le tissu à pois, le coton, le nylon, le polyester, le velours, le velours côtelé, la laine, la toile, la soie, l'argent, l'or, le cuir, le caoutchouc, le plastique, la fourrure.**

Provide students with small sheets of construction paper or tagboard (8 1/2 x 11), non-toxic glue sticks, scissors, old magazines (such as a clothing catalog).

Check with the home economics teacher or a local fabric store to see if they can give you a variety of fabric scraps. Remind students that they will be responsible for bringing most of their own materials. For some examples of materials that they don't find, they can use pictures from magazines (a plaid shirt, a wool coat, a silver necklace), but encourage them to use real materials as much as possible.

Once they have finished their collage, they should print the vocabulary word in large letters on the back of the visual. Collect the collages and show them to the class one at a time, asking the class to respond with the vocabulary word. A good collage should ellicit the correct response.

Next, divide the class into four groups, giving each group a few of the collages which they should place so everyone in the group can see them. Then have each student ask the group to point out a specific fabric, pattern or color. The members of the group then point out or touch the thing mentioned. When each member has participated in this activity, have the group exchange collages with another group and begin the drill again.

EXAMPLE:

STUDENT A:	**Montrez-moi le cuir brun.**
GROUP:	*(pointing to le cuir brun)* **Voici le cuir brun.**
STUDENT B:	**Montrez-moi le tissu à fleurs.**
GROUP:	**Voici le tissu à fleurs.**
STUDENT C:	**Montrez-moi la laine rouge.**
GROUP:	**Voici la laine rouge.**

Write the above dialog on the blackboard and do a few similar drills with the class as a large group before the small group work begins. When groups have finished their drills, collect the collages and post them in the classroom. Use these visuals again on review day.

3. PRÉSENTATION DE COLLECTIONS! (FASHION SHOW!)
(Unit 7 Lesson 25 pp. 346–350)

This activity targets most of the intelligences: the **bodily-kinesthetic** (modeling), the **linguistic** (creating the script), the **intrapersonal** (self-expression through modeling and creating the script), **interpersonal** (group activity), **spatial** (viewing the style show) and **musical** (use of background music).

■ To drill clothing and materials

Before beginning this activity, cover the material on pages 346–350. Divide the class into groups of three (two or four if necessary). One person in each group will be the narrator, the others will model. You might suggest that the students who speak French best be the narrators. Perhaps when you divide the class into groups, you might try to put one student in each group that has good pronunciation skills.

Give each group a copy of the instructions for modeling and writing their script that follows, and allow them time to prepare their script. Circulate and scan scripts for any errors. Help students with corrections. Help narrators with pronunciation if needed. Tell students to bring their clothes and accessories for the fashion show the next day. Bring some appropriate background music to play softly as students model.

After each group has given their presentation, ask the model to come forward as you ask comprehension questions on the script that was read.

> TEACHER: **De quelle couleur est son chapeau?**
>
> *(Call on individual students or the whole class.)*
> STUDENT: **Son chapeau est brun.**
> TEACHER: **Est-ce que cette chemise est en laine?**
> STUDENT: **Non, elle est en coton.**

Continue with the show and quiz students in this manner for the first half of the fashion show. For the last half, have each group do their presentation twice. The first time, the speaker narrates the entire script, with the models pointing out each item mentioned by touching the item or by motioning to it. The second time, the narrator will repeat the same script but will leave out the name of the article and will pause until the class fills in the clothing word. The model will be pointing out the article. The model will need to remember the order of the script in order to help the class figure out the words to use.

EXAMPLE: NARRATOR: **Barbara porte une _____.**

                              CLASS: **...jupe...**

                              NARRATOR: **...à fleurs et un _____.**

                              CLASS: **...chemisier.**

                              NARRATOR: **Il fait du soleil aujourd'hui et elle porte des...**

                              CLASS: **lunettes de soleil.**

Unité 7

INSTRUCTIONS FOR FASHION SHOW ACTIVITY

One person in your group is to be the narrator and will comment in French about what you are wearing. The entire group should work together to create the script. In deciding what to wear, you will need to choose clothing that you can easily put on top of what you wear to school or simply wear to school that day part of what you plan to model. You will not have time to leave the room to change clothes. Each model should wear a minimum of two **accessoires** (see p. 348) and at least three items from pages 346–347. The description of each model should include at least one mention of color, pattern and type of material (see p. 349).

You may have a theme to your part of the fashion show, modeling athletic clothes, winter clothes, clothes from a different culture or clothes from the fifties or sixties. You may write a simple script that basically describes what the models are wearing or you made add some original comments about the models. As the models are described they should point out or touch the clothing or accessory being described.

EXAMPLE #1

NARRATOR: **Monique porte un pull orange, un pantalon de laine, des chaussettes à fleurs et des chaussures. Elle porte un chapeau noir et un parapluie.**

EXAMPLE #2

NARRATOR: **Voici Monique. Elle va à l'école. Elle porte un parapluie parce qu'il pleut. Elle porte un pull orange, un pantalon de laine, des chaussettes à fleurs et des chaussures. Elle porte un sac de cuir. Monique est très à la mode, n'est-ce pas?**

4. LE COMPARATIF DES ADJECTIFS (Unit 7 Lesson 27 pp. 364–365)

These activities target the **spatial** and **bodily-kinesthetic** intelligences as students handle and look at objects. The **linguistic** intelligence is activated as students make up comparisons in French. The **logical-mathematical** intelligence is activated as students think of words in specific categories.

■ To Drill *Le comparatif des adjectifs*

After you have presented the material on page 364–365, drill the formation of comparisons with this activity. Bring some things to class that can be compared. For example, heavy things (cans of food, a bag of candy, a book); expensive things (pictures of appliances, furniture, rings, watches, clothing — a good source for these is a catalog; write the actual price on the back of the picture). Students may need to pick up these objects to judge weight and may need to look at them closely. If the weight or price is on the back or bottom of an object, just tell students not to look there.

Begin the drill with three objects that can be compared, such as expensive objects (**la bague, la montre, la chemise**). Call on a few students at random to get their opinion on the three objects. Tell them if their answers are correct.

STUDENT A:	**La bague est plus chère que la montre.**
TEACHER:	**Tu as raison.**
STUDENT B:	**La montre est aussi chère que la chemise.**
TEACHER:	**Non, tu n'as pas raison.**
STUDENT C:	**La montre est moins chère que la chemise.**
TEACHER:	**Tu as raison.**
STUDENT D:	**La chemise est aussi chère que la bague.**
TEACHER:	**Tu as raison.**

In putting together the three objects, try to pick two items that are the same weight or price and one item that is more or less expensive (or heavier). This way all three comparisons may be used. Challenge the students to come up with three correct comparisons. Write the correct comparisons down on the board as they are given.

Unité 7

This activity could also be done in small groups, with one student playing the role of the teacher. You would need several sets of objects but each group could pass them on to another group when they had finished with them.

After you've finished the first part of this activity, drill the comparative of **bon/bonne: meilleur/meilleure.** Name a category and ask a student to give an example from that category of something that is good. Then ask a few other students to mention something that is better. Before beginning this drill, write the different forms of **bon/meilleur** on the board.

EXAMPLE:

TEACHER: **Les sports**

STUDENT A: **Le jogging est bon.**

STUDENT B: **Le patinage est meilleur.**

STUDENT C: **La nation est meilleure.**

STUDENT D: **Le ski nautique est meilleur.**

TEACHER *(switch topic after a few responses):* **Les boissons.**

STUDENT A: **L'eau minérale est bonne.**

STUDENT B: **Le lait est meilleur.**

Other possible topics: **la viande, le dessert, les fruits, les films.** (Students might name a specific film or the kind of film—«**Les films policiers sont bons.**»)

5. *CELUI DE* + NOUN (Unit 7 Lesson 28 pp. 375–376)

This activity targets the **spatial** intelligence through the use of objects as visuals. The **linguistic** intelligence is targeted as students answer questions.

■ To Drill *Celui de* + noun *(ceux, celle, celles)*

Before beginning this activity, go over the material on pages 375–376. Then ask students to contribute an object for this drill (erasers, pens, notebooks, rings, photos, pencils, etc.). Ask them not to contribute earrings (too unsanitary) or any fragile items. Instruct students to try to conceal the object that they will be handing to you and to close their eyes as you walk around with a large paper bag to collect the items. (They can open their eyes when they are actually giving you the object.) Put a couple of your own objects into the bag before class starts. These should be plural objects (two papers, two rings).

Take the objects out of the bag one at a time (except for yours, which should be taken out two at a time). Hold up and name the object(s) and ask the class whose it is. Write part of this dialog on the blackboard as an example:

TEACHER:	**À qui est ce stylo?**
STUDENT A:	**C'est celui de Paul.**
PAUL *(if it is his)*:	**Oui, c'est mon stylo.**

(Return object to student as it's identified.)

TEACHER:	**À qui est la bague?**
STUDENT B:	**C'est celle de Monique.**
MONIQUE:	**Non, c'est celle de Marie.**

(Since the ring does not belong to Monique, she must name another student whose ring she thinks it is.)

MARIE:	**Oui, c'est ma bague.**
TEACHER:	**À qui sont les papiers?**
STUDENT C:	**Ce sont ceux de John.**
JOHN:	**Non, ce sont ceux du professeur.**
TEACHER:	**Oui, ce sont mes papiers.**

Continue this activity as long as you hold the interest of the class. If you have a large class you may not have time to drill all objects, in which case, simply return the remaining objects when you end the drill.

UNITÉ 8   BONNES VACANCES!

1. LA CONSTRUCTION VERBE + INFINITIF
(Unit 8 Lesson 30, pp. 414–415)

This activity targets the **intrapersonal** and **linguistic** intelligences as students write about themselves. The **bodily-kinesthetic** intelligence is activated as students pass papers and the **musical** intelligence when background music is played during the reading activity. The **interpersonal** intelligence is activated as students read and talk about each other.

■ To Drill *La construction verbe + infinitif*

Before beginning this activity, cover the material on pages 414 and 415. Then hand out the student worksheet for this activity and have students fill in the blanks. You might go over the meaning of each sentence (ask for volunteers to tell the class what each sentence means). Give students suggestions for filling in the blanks, helping them with vocabulary. Let them know that the entire class will be reading their papers. When everyone has finished filling in the blanks, have them begin passing their papers so that everyone will read all the papers. Tell students not to pass papers until you say: «**Passez les papiers.**» Ask the class a few comprehension questions before you have them pass their papers.

EXAMPLE:

TEACHER: **Qu'est-ce que John a appris cette année?**

STUDENT A *(who has John's paper):*   **Il a appris à danser.**

TEACHER: **Qui hésite à prendre des risques?**

STUDENT B *(who has Paula's paper):*   **Paula hésite à prendre des risques.**

STUDENT C: **Mark hésite à prendre des risques.**

TEACHER: **Qui rêve d'aller en France?**

STUDENT D: **Tom rêve d'aller en France.**

Have students pass their papers six or seven times with you asking questions. Then have them finish reading with no questions between readings. You might play some soft classical background music during this final reading period. Tell students to try to remember what they have read as you will be asking some questions at the end of the reading period. Students should read at their own pace and pass their paper on when ready but tell them not to hurry others. They can sit back, relax and listen to the music until a paper is sent their way. Collect the papers when everyone has read them. Mix them up and scan them, making up one question about each student's answers. The student you are referring to in the question should not answer unless the rest of the class is unable to come up with an answer.

EXAMPLE:

TEACHER: **Qui rêve d'aller en Italie?**

STUDENT: **Sara rêve d'aller en Italie.**

TEACHER: **Qu'est-ce que Monique oublie de faire?**

STUDENT: **Elle oublie de faire ses devoirs.**

Je m'appelle _____

Complete the following statements with an expression of your choice (some suggestions are given).

1. Je rêve d'aller _____ (en France, au Canada).

2. Cette année j'ai appris à _____ (jouer au tennis, danser).

3. Parfois j'oublie de _____ (faire mes devoirs, dire merci).

4. J'hésite à _____ (prendre des risques, manger des escargots).

5. Je refuse de manger _____ _(name a food)_.

6. L' année prochaine, je vais continuer à étudier _____ _(name a subject)_.

7. J'ai décidé de _____ (voyager, travailler, nager) pendant les grandes vacances.

8. Je voudrais apprendre à _____ (faire du ski nautique, parler japonais).

9. J'arrête d' étudier à _____ heures du soir.

10. Je voudrais réussir à jouer _____ (au basket, aux échecs, du piano, de la guitare).

Unité 8

2. L'USAGE DU FUTUR DANS LES PHRASES AVEC *SI*; L'USAGE DU FUTUR APRÈS *QUAND* (Unit 8 Lesson 31 p. 425–426)

This activity targets the **linguistic** and **logical-mathematical** intelligences as students complete sentences with logical words. The **spatial** and **bodily-kinesthetic** intelligences are activated as students give clues to their responses through drawings on the blackboard. The **intrapersonal** intelligence is activated through self-expression.

■ To Drill *L'usage du futur dans les phrases avec* si; *L'usage du futur après* quand

Before beginning this activity, cover the material on pages 425–426. Then hand out the student worksheet that follows. Have students fill in the blanks and tell them not to mention their answers to anyone. When everyone has finished, write the first sentence fragment on the board. Call one student forward to sketch what he or she wrote in the first blank. The class tries to guess what the sketch represents. When they say the correct word, the student who drew the sketch responds, **«Oui»** and then repeats the entire sentence: **«S'il fait beau, j'irai à la plage.»** Whoever has the same answer replies; **«Moi aussi, j'irai à la plage.»** Students that have the same answers will not be asked to sketch that particular answer.

Continue having students come to the board to draw their sketches until all answers for sentence number one have been covered. Continue in the same way for the rest of the sentences. Remember to write the key sentence on the board each time you begin working with a sentence. **(Si j'ai assez d'argent, j'achèterai . . .).** Make sure everyone gets a chance to do at least one drawing. At the end of the activity, ask each student to make one statement that pertains to another student. The verbs will need to be changed to the **il** or **elle** form.

EXAMPLE: **Si Marnie a soif, elle boira une limonade.**

This activity could also be done in small groups. In which case, do the first two sentences as examples with the large group and then divide the class into small groups. Each group will need access to a small portion of the board or some sheets of large construction paper and some non-toxic color markers.

Je m'appelle _____

Complete the following sentences:

1. S'il fait beau, j'irai _____.

2. Si j'ai assez d'argent, j'achèterai _____.

3. Si j'ai soif, je boirai _____.

4. Si j'ai faim, je mangerai _____.

5. Si je vais en France, je verrai _____.

6. Quand j'irai à l'université, j'étudierai _____.

7. Quand j'aurai 30 ans, j'habiterai à _____.

8. Quand je serai dans le Colorado, je _____.

9. Quand je serai en Californie, je _____.

Unité 8

3. LE CONDITIONNEL DANS LES PHRASES AVEC *SI*

(Unit 8 Lesson 32 p. 435)

This activity targets the **musical** and **linguistic** intelligences as students sing a song.

■ To Drill *Le conditionnel dans les phrases avec* si

Before presenting this song, cover the material on page 435. If you are not musical, ask a few musical students to work on it and present it to the class. The melody is *Il Peut, Bergère.*

Si j'étais à Paris

1. Si j'étais à Paris,
   Si j'étais à Paris,
   Je parlerais français à tout le monde.
   Je parlerais français à tout le monde, la la!
   Je parlerais français — français à tout le monde.

2. Si j'étais à Paris,
   Si j'étais à Paris,
   J'achèterais du vin et un petit pain.
   J'achèterais du vin et un petit pain, la la!
   J'achèterais du vin et un petit pain, petit pain.

3. Si j'étais à Paris,
   Si j'étais à Paris,
   J'irais voir le Louvre et Notre-Dame.
   J'irais voir le Louvre et Notre-Dame, la la!
   J'irais voir le Louvre, le Louvre et Notre-Dame.

UNITÉ 9   BONNE ROUTE

1. LA VOITURE   (Unit 9 Lesson 33 p. 460)

> These activities target the **bodily-kinesthetic** and **spatial** intelligences as students learn the vocabulary through gestures and drawing. The **linguistic** intelligence is also targeted as students say the words.

■ To Drill *La voiture*

Go over the pronunciation of the words on page 460, then drill the car vocabulary using TPR. Assign a word to each student and have him or her think of an appropriate gesture (or simply photocopy and cut up the list of words and gestures on the next page and and give each student one). Students might make up an original gesture or use the suggested gesture.

Have the class stand in a circle. Begin by saying each word on the list and having the class repeat the word after you. Then the student who was assigned this word gives the gesture. You say the word again and the entire class repeats the word and the accompanying gesture. Tell the class you will keep repeating the word until you see everyone doing the gesture. Then go on to the next word, continuing the drill in the same manner until you have covered all the words. Then ask each student to give the gesture for his or her word. Have the class respond with the word. Finally, ask each individual student to say the target word and have the class respond with the gesture.

SUGGESTED GESTURES

l'essence   Hold nose as if smelling gas fumes.

un pneu   Act as if pumping up a tire with a tire pump.

le coffre   Pretend you are turning key in trunk, then lift trunk.

le réservoir   Pretend to unscrew and take off gas cap.

le toit   Move a flat hand back and forth over your head, eyes glancing up.

le siège   Squat as if sitting down.

la ceinture de sécurité   Pretend to fasten a seatbelt.

la porte   Pretend to open a car door.

le clignotant   Blink your right or left eye.

le capot   Pretend to squeeze the release latch and lift the hood.

le moteur   Cup hand behind ear as if listening to the motor.

le phare   Lean head back and squint as if blinded by headlights.

une roue   Act as if you're kicking a tire.

le rétroviseur   Pretend you're looking in the rear view mirror and adjusting it.

le klaxon   Make movements with your right hand as if pressing on the horn.

le volant   Pretend you are holding on to a steering wheel with both hands and make movements as if turning the wheel.

le pare-brise   Make a circular flat hand motion as if you are cleaning the windshield.

le frein   Pretend you have your hands on the steering wheel, lean forward, lift right foot moving it a bit to the left and press to the floor.

l'accélérateur   Pretend you have your hands on the steering wheel, press right foot to the floor and lean body backwards.

la clé   Gesture as if turning the key in the ignition.

un essuie-glace   Extend arms forward, bent at the elbows at right angles, move forearms back and forth to simulate windshield wipers.

To further drill this vocabulary, ask for a few volunteers to go to the blackboard and draw a car as the rest of the class describes it. Tell students they may draw any type of car they want. Call on individuals to name the part of the car to be drawn. For example, if a students says «**les phares**», the students at the board would draw the headlights. If students at the board do not understand the word given, they should turn around and look at the class. The class should then give the gesture for this word.

Have students continue giving vocabulary words until the car is finished. Then have the "artists" sit down. Call on four other students to come to the board. Tell them that these cars have been poorly made and are falling apart. Ask each member of the class to mention a car part. When each car part is mentioned, the students at the board erase that part of the car. Continue this activity until all of the car has been erased.

2. LE SUBJONCTIF: FORMATION RÉGULIÈRE
(Unit 9 Lesson 35 pp. 472-475)

> This game targets the **logical-mathematical** intelligence as clues are given so students can figure out words in specific categories. The **interpersonal** intelligence is targeted with a group activity and the **linguistic** intelligence is activated through reading, speaking and listening.

Before you begin this game, cover the material on pages 272–275. Divide the class into two groups. Have two members from Group A come forward. They will give clues to their group in French to help them guess a certain place, profession, etc. Their group has one minute to guess the answers. Then it is Group B's turn. One point is scored for each correct answer. The team with the most points wins. Be sure that each team has an equal number of chances to give clues. Hand out the clue sheets when students come forward to give clues. Give students a minute to read the sheet of clues before they begin.

EXAMPLE:

Two students from Group A receive clue sheet *places*. Group A is told that the category is places. The two students will give clues as to what one must do in each location. You might write the following on the blackboard as an example.

TWO STUDENTS: **Il faut que nous écoutions le docteur.**
Il faut que nous nous reposions.

GROUP A: **L'hôpital.**

TWO STUDENTS: **Oui.**

(Students then go on to describe the next word. Words do not have to be described in the order they appear.)

Have a student from the opposite team keep track of the time. When one minute is up, the time keeper says "Stop." Then it is the other team's turn to give clues. Two students from Group B receive a clue sheet and give their clues.

Make a copy of the clue sheets on the following pages. Instruct students to use the clues on the clue sheet but also to make up clues of their own.

When the game is over, collect the clue sheets and read the answers one at a time. Ask individuals in the class to give you some of the clues they heard.

EXAMPLE:

TEACHER:	**L'école.**
STUDENT A:	**Il faut étudier.**
STUDENT B:	**Il faut écouter les professeurs.**

CLUE SHEET 1: PLACES

We will describe what we must do in these places. You need to guess the place.

(à l'école)

Il faut que nous étudions.

Il faut que nous écoutions les professeurs.

Il faut que nous...

(au stade)

Il faut que nous aimions les sports.

Il faut que nous soyons en forme.

Il faut que nous ...

(à la plage)

Il faut que nous nagions.

Il faut que nous portions des lunettes de soleil.

Il faut que nous...

(à la bibliothèque)

Il faut que nous lisions.

Il faut que nous ne parlions pas beaucoup.

Il faut que nous...

(à l'hôpital)

Il faut que nous écoutions le docteur.

Il faut que nous obéissions à l'infirmière.

Il faut que nous ...

(au restaurant)

Il faut que nous donnions un pourboire au garçon.

Il faut que nous mangions.

Il faut que nous...

CLUE SHEET 2: PLACES

We will describe what we must do in these places. You need to guess the place.

(dans une voiture)
Il faut que nous conduisions bien.
Il faut que nous mettions le clignotant.
Il faut que nous…

(dans une ferme)
Il faut que nous donnions à manger aux animaux.
Il faut que nous plantions des plantes.
Il faut que…

(dans la cuisine)
Il faut que nous mettions le lait dans le réfrigérateur.
Il faut que nous mettions la table.
Il faut que nous…

(dans une classe de musique)
Il faut que nous chantions.
Il faut que nous jouions du piano.
Il faut que nous…

(dans une classe de français)
Il faut que nous parlions français.
Il faut que nous lisions français.
Il faut que nous…

(dans la salle de bains)
Il faut que nous nous lavions les cheveux.
Il faut que nous nous brossions les dents.
Il faut que nous…

CLUE SHEET 3: PEOPLE

We are going to describe to you what certain people might typically say. You need to guess who might say these things.

(une mère)

Il faut que tu mettes la table.

Il faut que tu mettes un manteau.

Il faut que tu...

(un professeur)

Il faut que tu me donnes les devoirs.

Il faut que tu études.

Il faut que tu...

(un dentiste)

Il faut que tu te brosses les dents.

Il faut que tu ouvres la bouche.

Il faut que tu ...

(un ami)

Il faut que tu me dises «Salut!»

Il faut que tu m'invites à la fête.

Il faut que tu...

(un professeur de musique)

Il faut que tu chantes bien.

Il faut que tu pratiques de la flûte.

Il faut que tu . ..

(un élève)

Il faut que je finisse mes devoirs.

Il faut que j'étudie ce soir.

Il faut que je...

CLUE SHEET 4: FOODS

We will describe what we must buy to make a certain dish. You need to tell us what dish we are most likely making.

(un sandwich au jambon)
Il faut que nous achetions du pain.
Il faut que nous achetions du jambon.
Il faut que nous ...

(une salade de légumes)
Il faut que nous achetions des tomates.
Il faut que nous achetions des carottes.
Il faut que nous ...

(des crêpes)
Il faut que nous achetions des oeufs.
Il faut que nous achetions du lait.
Il faut que nous ...

(une tarte aux fruits)
Il faut que nous achetions des fruits.
Il faut que nous achetions du sucre.
Il faut que nous ...

(un croque-monsieur)
Il faut que nous achetions du fromage.
Il faut que nous achetions du jambon.
Il faut que nous ...

(une omelette aux champignons)
Il faut que nous achetions des oeufs.
Il faut que nous achetions des champignons.
Il faut que nous ...

CLUE SHEET 5: PROFESSIONS

We will describe things people must do in certain professions. Try to name the profession.

(un secrétaire)

Il faut qu'il travaille dans un bureau.

Il faut qu'il écrive des lettres.

Il faut qu'il …

(une photographe)

Il faut qu'elle prenne des photos.

Il faut qu'elle achète un appareil-photo.

Il faut qu'elle …

(un mannequin)

Il faut qu'elle porte de nouveaux vêtements.

Il ne faut pas qu'elle mange beaucoup.

Il faut qu'elle …

(une programmeuse)

Il faut qu'elle utilise un ordinateur.

Il faut qu'elle travaille dans un bureau.

Il faut qu'elle …

(un professeur)

Il faut qu'il enseigne.

Il faut qu'il travaille dans une salle de classe.

Il faut qu'il …

(une infermière)

Il faut qu'elle aide les malades.

Il faut qu'elle travaille dans un hôpital.

Il faut qu'elle …

CLUE SHEET 6: SPORTS

We are going to describe what you must do to participate in certain sports. Try to guess the sports.

(la natation)

Il faut que vous portiez un maillot de bain.

Il faut que vous nagiez.

Il faut que vous …

(le tennis)

Il faut que vous utilisiez une raquette.

Il faut que vous jouiez un match.

Il faut que vous …

(le volley)

Il faut que vous jouiez un match.

Il faut que vous jouiez avec un ballon.

Il faut que vous …

(le ski)

Il faut que vous aimiez la neige.

Il faut que vous portiez des gants.

Il faut que vous …

(le jogging)

Il faut que vous couriez.

Il faut que vous portiez des tennis.

Il faut que vous …

(le ping-pong)

Il faut que vous utilisiez une table.

Il faut que vous jouiez avec une raquette.

Il faut que …

3. LE SUBJONCTIF: FORMATION IRRÉGULIÈRE

(Unit 9 Lesson 36 pp.480–481)

This activity activates the **intrapersonal** and **linguistic** intelligences as students write paragraphs expressing their opinions. The **interpersonal** intelligence is activated through a group activity in which students share what they've written. The **musical** intelligence is activated as background music is played during the writing activity.

■ To Drill *Le subjonctif: formation irrégulière*

Before beginning this activity, go over the material on pages 480–481. Copy the student worksheet that follows and have students complete it. Give students class time to work on their compositions. Play soft classical background music during the writing period. If some students finish before others, you might read their work and circle any mistakes and have them make corrections. When all students have finished, divide the class into groups of five or six. One member of each group will take a tally of the responses. This person will note the two characteristics most often mentioned by the group for each subject.

Student A starts out by slowly reading aloud one of the paragraphs, pausing after each statement. If any other group member has the same response, he or she indicates this.

EXAMPLE:

STUDENT A *(reading paragraph 1):* **Un bon professeur.**
          Il faut qu'il soit intelligent. (pause)

STUDENT B: **Moi aussi, je dis qu'il faut qu'il soit intelligent.**

STUDENT C: **Moi aussi, je dis qu'il faut qu'il soit intelligent.**

STUDENT A *(continuing if there are no more responses):*
          Il faut qu'il aime enseigner.

The person keeping the tally writes down the phrases and marks how many students in the group had the same response. (It will not be necessary to record any phrases that only one person wrote.) When Student A has finished reading the paragraph, Student B reads any sentences left in his or her paragraph.

Students should cross out any of their sentences that match what someone else has read.

These directions are a bit complicated. You might want to write the above dialog on the blackboard and go over it with the students before you put them into groups. Once they are in groups, circulate to make sure the groups are on task.

Reading continues around the group until all paragraphs about **un bon professeur** are read. This activity continues with paragraph #2, **Un bon élève**. When everyone in the group has read all four paragraphs and tallies have been taken, the group chooses one person to report the results to the large group. Before beginning the large group activity, all small groups must be ready. Ask one student in each group to tell the class their two most popular responses for each subject. After you have all the responses for subject #1 (**un bon professeur**), continue in like manner for the rest of the subjects.

EXAMPLE:

TEACHER: **Un bon professeur**

GROUP A: **Il faut qu'il soit intelligent. Il faut qu'il aime enseigner.**

GROUP B: **Il faut qu'il soit intelligent. Il faut qu'il soit gentil.**

Je m'appelle _____

Complete these paragraphs describing what you think one must do to be a good teacher, a good student, a good friend and a good millionaire. Remember to use the subjunctive form of the verb following **Il faut que**.

#1 Un bon professeur

Il faut qu'il (être) _____.

Il faut qu'il _____.

Il faut qu'il _____.

Il faut qu'il _____.

#2 Un bon élève

Il faut qu'il (être) _____.

Il faut qu'il (faire) _____.

Il faut qu'il (aller) _____.

Il faut qu'il _____.

#3 Un bon ami

Il faut qu'il (être) _____.

Il faut qu'il _____.

Il faut qu'il _____.

Il faut qu'il _____.

#4 Un bon millionnaire

Il faut qu'il (avoir) _____.

Il faut qu'il (être) _____.

Il faut qu'il _____.

Il faut qu'il _____.